IS IT JUST ME OR IS

**THE WHINGER'S GUIDE
TO SOUTH AFRICA
From AA to JZ**

EVERYTHING

KAK?

GW00383052

"A great – and possibly psychologically vital – book for South African emotional health"
— *The Mercury*

"This is far more than just a whinger's guide to life in this post-democratic South Africa. It's a jam-packed, well-researched compendium of facts and figures put together in such a clever, wry, witty way that you'll be laughing (even when you should be crying)"
— *Arja Salafranca, The Star*

"Insightful, razor-sharp… A fantastically funny read – perfect for making you realise when you're being a grumpy pessimist"
— *Men's Health*

"[Kak] quite splendidly takes the piss out of South Africa… We don't have nearly enough of this kind of writing"
— *Leon de Kock, Sunday Times*

"This is a very funny book, but perhaps not what you want to give your mother-in-law. Tim Richman and Grant Schreiber hit the button for me on just about every whinge they came up with, and they came up with a few… This is truly a book I recommend"
— *Tina Weavind, The Times*

Hysterically funny commentary on South Africa – as we know it"
— *Samantha Cowen, Highveld Radio*

"Every whinger's Bible"
    — *Roekeloos.co.za*

"A bad-tempered, foul-mouthed, unconstructive review of the state of the Rainbow Nation a few years on… In short: if you've recently emigrated to Perth, drive an SUV, wear Crocs, are a Sharks fan, or heaven forbid, a Paris Hilton fan, speak on a cellphone in the cinema, go cycling in pink Lycra budgie-smugglers and/or prick the boerie, this book is not for you — unless, indeed, you are exactly who it's for. If you're none of these, buy the book anyway: you're bound to find a whinge or two to share… It will reinforce your prejudices, reassure you that it's Other People's fault — but also perhaps make you wonder whether you're not one of the Other People. So you'll enjoy it and it will be good for you — which is an odd but welcome effect of all that whingeing"
    — *Michiel Heyns, Sunday Independent*

"Hugely entertaining"
    — *News24*"

"This is a refreshingly honest and hilarious collection of things to whinge about, catering especially for the South African male. It is at times a political rant, and at times quite trivial, but always funny"
    — *The Citizen*

"Excellent book. Love it. Brilliant"
    — *Sasha Martinengo, 5fm*

Published by Two Dogs
an imprint of SchreiberFord Publications and Struik Publishers

•

SchreiberFord Publications
PO Box 50664, The Waterfront, Cape Town, 8001

Struik Publishers
(a division of New Holland Publishing (South Africa) (Pty) Ltd)
PO Box 1144, Cape Town, 8000
New Holland Publishing is a member of Avusa Ltd

•

First published 2007
Reprinted 2008 (three times)
5 7 9 8 6 4

•

Publication © 2007 Two Dogs
Text © 2007 Tim Richman, Grant Schreiber

•

All rights reserved. No part of this publication may be reproduced, stored
in a retrieval system or transmitted, in any form or by any means, electronic,
mechanical, photocopying, recording or otherwise, without the prior
written permission of the copyright owners.

•

Publishing director: Daniel Ford
Managing creative director: Grant Schreiber
Publishing manager and editor: Tim Richman
Art director: Francois Pretorius

•

Reproduction by Hirt & Carter Cape (Pty) Ltd
Printed and bound by Paarl Print, Oosterland Street, Paarl, South Africa

•

ISBN 978 1 92013 720 5
info@twodogs.co.za
www.twodogs.co.za

Huskies with their tongues out

About the authors

Tim Richman is an editor and writer. He is co-author of
Don't Climb Kilimanjaro… Climb The Ruwenzori and
Why I'll Never Live In Oz Again.

Grant Schreiber is a publisher and company director.
He is co-author of *My Dad – By South African Sons.*

Both have been known to whinge a bit.

Acknowledgments

Thanks to Julie Rowand, Rupert Butler, Steve Connolly, Alison
de Villiers, Mike Dixon, Heather Irvine, Francois Pretorius,
Kerry Rogers, Ania Rokita, Li Sowdon, Chris Warncke and
the Cedarberg crew – who have all also been known to whinge
on occasion.

Special thanks to the SASASU men – who will one day take over
the world.

Dedicated to unrecognised USB flash drives everywhere.

Introduction

Welcome to *Is It Just Me Or Is Everything Kak? The Whinger's Guide To South Africa*. As the title and subtitle might suggest, there is a reasonable amount of whingeing in this book. We even have a go at whingers once or twice. Nothing irony can't excuse, of course, but that's what you're dealing with. So you know.

Now, to give you a heads up, we're not actually offering too many solutions to the kakness that permeates our daily lives, although we have considered trying to get everything listed here banned. Back in the dark days of apartheid, the Nats used this approach on pornographic magazines, subversive thoughts, black people and the like, but unfortunately it can be impractical at times and it's bound to throw up the odd stickler. Danny K, for one, would almost definitely not go along with it. And nix telling Kobus Wiese he's banned. Plus we've tried banning crime and that's not working out too well (despite what some people may think). So banning's out. Think we'll just whinge, then.

Anyway, just to assure you that we actually think South Africa is a pretty good place. It's certainly no kakker than the rest of the world. Things are nice here, in fact. It's just that, sometimes, they're nice and kak.

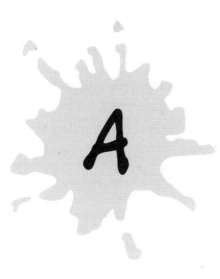

AA

Just to be clear: it's not the car club we're talking about here, or the boozers' support group; it's the race-related employment policy. We thought we'd go with the ambiguous header just so it could kick things off – because we wouldn't want to start with a topic that doesn't get down your shorts and chafe a bit.

Black or white, every South African in the job market has an opinion on affirmative action. And, somehow, that opinion always ends up... down someone else's shorts.

"AA policies are necessary to uplift underprivileged, 'previously disadvantaged' black South Africans from generations of repression and lack of opportunity..." Chafe.

"Affirmative action is based on the colour of a person's skin – hence, it is as racist as any apartheid policy..." Chafe chafe.

"South African business hierarchy resembles a cappuccino – black on the bottom, white above, with a sprinkling of black right at the top. Without employment equity it will always be like this..." Chafe chafe chafe chafe chafe chafe chafe chafe chafe chafe...

Maybe it's the cynical application of AA legislation by window-dressing big-money corporations that rubs you up the wrong way; or perhaps it's the fact that you've been told "pale male, bottom of the scale" by your recruitment agent. Or it could be the huffy white boys fresh out of varsity complaining that jobs aren't just landing in their laps any more; or the way affirmative action has been implemented with far more enthusiasm and good intention than common sense and forethought. For many, it's the great, big irony that those who suffer the most due to the failure of basic service delivery are the poorest of the poor – that is, the previously disadvantaged who are supposed to be benefiting the most.

For me, it's the bloody wait in the queue at Home Affairs.

Accounts departments

"Speak to Accounts" – a sentence to send a shiver of unmitigated fear down any mortal's spine, for those in the employ of the accounts department are anything but mortal. Black-hearted ghouls and hideous beasts from the fiery cauldrons of hell, more like, whose only job requirements are an unsightly appearance and the ability to make you feel like an apologetic vagrant just because you've asked to receive your IRP5 *before* the personal-tax submission date. Unlike last year.

Agents

Few people know this, but the term "agent" is actually an abbreviation of the phrase "agent of the devil". Yes, this is true. And it's quite logical if you think about it. Estate agents, recruitment agents, celebrity agents – they have no soul, morals or conscience, hence they are clearly minions of the Prince Of Darkness. The least evil of all agents are secret agents; as in the people who spend years learning the dark arts of espionage in order to assassinate, murder and maim without conscience. Those other agents: far worse.

Note that travel agents are not necessarily pure evil, as such, but they make up for this through sheer incompetence.

Airline weight allowances

Of the many factors that can contribute to making air travel a thoroughly unpleasant experience – the queues, the delays, the body-search violations, SAA – the two worst must surely be excess-baggage costs and sitting next to fat people.

Having to pay extra because your bag is over the permissible weight might be understandable if the fuel-to-weight ratios were as critical as when, say, a rocket ship is sent into lunar orbit. But they are not – as is clearly evident when you see the inevitable selection of gargantuan passengers gravitating towards your airline counter. Here I am paying a R48,000 fine for being a couple of kilograms overweight, and there's Larry Lardass checking in his titanic butt without any penalties. It's an outrage! Given the current ludicrous arrangement that sees a 130kg wideload with 20kg of luggage in the clear, while a 60kg woman carrying 30kg has to take out a second mortgage just so she can bring her makeup kit on holiday, it defies logic that passengers aren't weighed together with their bags like they were in the good old days. If this gets *me* steaming, I can't imagine how the anorexic chicks must be feeling.

Oh the cruel irony of those fateful flights when you're pinged for an overweight suitcase and then get seated between a couple of heffalumps for 11 hours. Naturally, they both fall into catatonic sleep within seconds of inhaling the first meal, leaving you trapped and cowering while your TV screen malfunctions and a teething baby wails away in front of you. As flabby arm-rolls close in on you from both flanks, invading your miniscule territory, engine failure is just a heartbeat away.

American English

Where to start? How about "deplane". As in *Thank you for flying Crappy American Airlines; please allow geriatrics and the grotesquely obese to deplane before you.*

You don't "plane"! So why would you deplane? (NB: It's embark and disembark.)

Or "burglarize". As in *At this present moment in time it would seem apparent that criminals have burglarized the bank. Police are on the lookout for several Hispanic men driving a Chev pickup, which the men utilized in the burglarization.* Burgled, Americans, it's burgled.

And FYI, it's "aluminium". And the word "gotten" does not exist. And where the hell did you come up with "winningest"? And lose the Zs. And stop messing around with our spell checks. And sort out your foreign policy.

The ANC

Right, so here's a party with so much political goodwill and leverage in its back pocket after half a century of apartheid (on the back of several centuries of colonial oppression) that only the Holocaust can justifiably generate more universal sympathy. Moral high ground? You bet. Then, in Nelson Mandela, they have a man who comes to symbolise leadership, nation building and greatness: an icon of our times, a bringer of peace and reconciliation, one of the most widely celebrated and admired people in recent history. It seems near on impossible to cock this up.

That was a few years ago now…

Since Madiba stepped down, the ANC has seemingly done all in its power to reverse its holy image, as its underlings have all fussed about, scrambling over each other to get to the top of the pile. Externally and internally, the ANC seems permanently mired in bad press. Hardly a day goes by that a minor or major controversy doesn't need quashing.

The allegations fly regularly – who knows what's true or not? – and the responses are as inconsistent as can be. The deputy president is in a "generally corrupt" relationship with his financial advisor. Fired. The deputy minister of health is embarrassing her boss (by doing her job competently). Fired. The national director of public prosecutions isn't toeing the line. Fired. The health minister is incompetent, an alcoholic and a thief. Not fired. Five senior MPs commit travel fraud. Not fired. The national commissioner of the South African Police Service has personal links with a high-profile crime kingpin implicated in murder and drug smuggling. Not fired.

Somebody stop the madness!

The double standards are mind-blowing. Let's have some of the integrity and honesty back, please – instead of the unpunished corruption and never-ending squabbling between internal factions, all with their own agendas: the Mbeki bloc, the Zuma bloc, the BEE boys, the ANC Women's League, the ANC Youth League, Cosatu, the SACP. Even within these factions, they can't stop bickering. Just ask Willy Madisha.

Possibly the most infuriating behaviour of the party at the moment is its refusal to accept criticism in any form, as typified by National Assembly speaker Baleka Mbete's decision to eject DA member Mike Waters from parliament in September 2007 for "offensive and unbecoming language" when he asked whether Manto Tshabalala-

Msimang's history of thievery was known to the president. Apparently any words critical of the ANC are "offensive and unbecoming".

Having spent several years doing a piss-poor job of running Cape Town, the party's Western Cape branch couldn't even accept the valid municipal victory – in democratic elections – of the DA in 2006. Presumably it expected Capetonians to be satisfied with its mere presence in power. When they weren't, and the ANC found itself ousted, it resorted repeatedly to underhand tactics to reclaim power.

With minister of defence Mosiuoa Lekota on record as saying his party would not rest until "every member of the South African public is an ANC member", the blurring of country and party interests seems to be the guiding rule at the moment. You get the feeling that the party head honchos will only be happy with the state of the nation when it becomes entirely ANC-run. The thing is it doesn't need to go that far: the ANC only requires 75 per cent of the MPs in parliament to be able to change the constitution. They could then, if they wished, decide to stop holding regular democratic elections. And pass laws that blacks should not only get preference in job placements but be legally permitted to assume positions currently occupied by whites. And that the movement of whites should be regulated by means of a specially produced identification tag or passbook, if you will…

Very *Animal Farm*, this.

A nice metaphor to conclude: at a policy conference in July 2007, there was an entrance for ordinary delegates, an entrance for VIPs, another entrance for VVIPs and yet another entrance for the real big-cheese VVVIPs. Really. And this is the party for the people?

Arguing

What is it with people these days that no-one wants to debate a topic? "It's my way or the highway" seems to be the incongruous collective mantra. No compromise, no concession, no "I take your point, good sir". Or even the occasional "Touché".

Rather it's, "You're wrong, asshole! And you're an idiot! And everything about you is stupid!" The responses on both sides of the argument are as automated as Pavlov's dog. It's like ringing a bell.

"Hey Avi, you see some Palestinian kids were killed yesterday when they were 'accidentally' shelled by IDF tanks?" Ding-ding. "Screw you, man! We had to survive the Holocaust! Those Palestinians would wipe us off the face of the earth if they could!"

"Hey, Yusuf, you see Hezbollah fired some more rockets into Haifa again, killing innocent Israeli women and children?" Ding-ding. "The Jews started it! They kicked us out of our homeland and have treated us like animals ever since!"

This kind of dialogue is typified in South Africa by the regular newspaper correspondence between apparently eternal Palestinian sympathiser Ronnie Kasrils and angry people from Sea Point with surnames like Cohen and Rabinowitzbergstein. But it's everywhere else, too. Other never-ending arguments in which the antagonists just don't listen to each other: atheists v the religious; Creationism v evolution; Big Oil v climate change; affirmative action v anti-affirmative action; pro-nuclear v anti-nuclear; pro-choice v anti-abortion; pro-America v anti-America; rugby v football; the Hoff v Chuck Norris. And on and on.

Occasionally, just occasionally, a hardline stance is justifiable. Such as the Paris-Hilton-must-die lobby. Fair enough. Justified. No point in debating that one – it would just lead to delays. But is it too much to ask that people, especially those in influential and powerful positions (ahem, Ronnie Kasrils), actually consider both sides of the question before spewing out their destructive bile? You know, maybe concede a point. Every now and then.

The Australian cricket team

In the context of this book, the Australian cricket team most certainly is not "kak". What is kak, however, is the way the Aussies always bring their A-game when they play South Africa, and we always… don't. Well, very rarely, then.

Since we returned to international cricket in 1992, there have at least been a couple of high points against them. Let's see, there was the legendary 1994 Sydney test match, with the most joyous caught-and-bowled ever. And, more recently, the 438 match at the Wanderers, which was just insane. So that's nice.

Besides that, though, the situation is dire. Given that the Proteas have generally been near the top of both the test and one-day rankings – barring the odd dry spell – you'd think we would at least give the Australians a fair run for their money. Eh, not so much.

As of late 2007, we had three other test victories to go with 15 mostly enormous losses and a handful of draws; and 28 ODI wins from 67 starts. That last stat is not wholly embarrassing given the fact that the Aussies are three-time consecutive World Champions, but then you think about the matches that actually counted for something… and that explains why the Aussies are three-time consecutive World Champions.

Sigh.

We've come this far and it's pretty depressing, so let's get on to some personal stats, shall we? Here's a comparison of test-match averages between a couple of South Africa's most capped and highest-ranked players in recent years and a couple of Australia's:

Jacques Kallis
Test-match batting average against all opposition: high 50s
Average against Australia: 38.32
Shaun Pollock
Test-match bowling average against all opposition: low 20s
Average against Australia: 36.85
Ricky Ponting
Test-match batting average against all opposition: just under 60
Average against South Africa: 63.95
Shane Warne
Test-match bowling average against all opposition: 25.41
Average against South Africa: 24.16

The conclusion here is rather straightforward. Our boys fall apart when it comes to the most meaningful, important opposition – the one team that all South Africans live to see beaten – while the Aussies either perform to their normal high standards against us or they actually play better than they do against other, weaker teams.

Damn you, convicts. Why don't you ever perform against us the way you nearly lost to Bangladesh that one time?

Bank fees

Let's say you bank at Absa. It seems, on the surface, to be a decent enough financial institution. Secure, good reputation, sponsors the Springboks *and* the PSL, nice multiracial marketing campaigns – all you would hope for from your trusted bank.

Then, if you take a whirl through the Absa website, you might note that the company considers its customers to be "the cornerstone" of its business. "We seek to meet your financial needs by offering quality financial advice, products and services," the customer charter boldly declares. "[W]e consistently strive to 'walk the talk' and exceed your expectations by anticipating and meeting your needs".

What a steaming load of cock custard.

After all that pretty website fluffery, the telling words appear on my bank statement:

INTERNET BANK FEE	-101.95
SERVICE FEE	-52.75
TRANSACTION CHARGE	-17.40
ADMIN CHARGE	-16.40
OD: LEDGER	-15.00

That's more than R200 a month on bank fees for one teeny tiny account. In other words, I give Absa close to R2,500 a year so that it can play with my money. Indeed, that does exceed my expectations. By rather a long way. Especially considering Absa and the other major South African banks have all *reduced* their banking fees since April 2007 due to increasing customer dissatisfaction. Now, instead of being utterly outraged at the way our banks take advantage of us, we can just be mildly appalled. Although, when I compare my new reduced rates with overseas rates – less than R30 a month for an equivalent Australian account or, get this, absolutely zero for a UK account – the outrage returns. Then add on the point that the R200-a-month figure assumes I'm not using other banks' ATMs, with their exorbitant Saswitch charges, and, well, there's even more outrage. Clearly, the reason why its customers are the cornerstone of Absa's business is because it takes so much money from them.

The good news about Saswitch fees, which can treble the cost of an ATM transaction, is that, as of midway through 2007, South African banks were considering a proposal to scrap the "premium" Saswitch charge and let customers get away with paying a far smaller carriage fee for using another bank's infrastructure. If this proposal is passed, bank customers stand to save R500 million a year on ATM charges. R500 million! That's how much we are currently being screwed over every year for Saswitch charges alone. And the bad news? This proposal was first suggested in 2001. So don't hold your breath. And don't think they're not going to try screw you over in other ways.

The ultimate example of the relentless abuse-the-customer attitude of South African banks is the "insufficient funds" decline fee. You're so broke that you cannot even draw money from the ATM – and then they "anticipate and meet your needs" by charging you for it. Those sick, twisted bastards.

Despite all this, I would be content with my bank's criminal fee structuring if all similarly rapacious financial institutions were, by legislation, impelled to have the words "Blood-sucking motherfuckers" spray-painted on their branch windows. That would make it okay.

BEE

Listen to controversial Employment Equity Commission chairman Jimmy Manyi for around 15 seconds, say, and it's quite likely you'll want to execute a swift kick to his groin, followed by a hand-strike to the neck. "Judoooo CHOP!" you might cry as you beat him to the ground, before delivering a dance of joy over his prostrate body...

When you wake up, however, you will find that, back in reality, Manyi is still active and influential and pronouncing, in his rather vociferous way, all manner of controversial – and what could be construed as racist – comments. In fact, if you are white, which I am, it is highly likely you will construe them as racist comments. Then again, South African employment equity was never really for my benefit, and as annoying as the man is, he's not really the problem. If there wasn't a Jimmy Manyi, there would be a Jimmy Manyo or a Timmy Manyi or a Manyi Manyi... Like Judgment Day in the *Terminator* movies, Jimmy Manyi is inevitable.

So we have to breathe deeply, resist the kneejerk cock shot and get on to the problem at hand. In this case, Black Economic Empowerment.

It has been written that Black Economic Empowerment is "a growth strategy, targeting the South African economy's weakest point: inequality". That is all well and good. But as is standard practice with any race-related issue in South Africa – which is to say, practically any issue in South Africa (see **Racial obsessing**) – it is not so much the intention of the policy as its execution that causes the widespread vexation.

When you consider a hugely successful Cyril Ramaphosa type arriving at a board meeting for a multibillion-rand corporation in his shiny black Merc CL 600, you have a vision of what could be in South Africa: a land of economic opportunities for all, irrespective of skin colour. But then you consider him racing off to another eight meetings that day because he's on 62 different boards, along with the four other high-powered BEE kingpins out there (there's Cyril, Patrice, Tokyo... er, I'm battling here) – and you realise that the inequality is going nowhere. In other words, there's a lot of hoo-ha and not much progress.

Big-line-up concerts
Months of hype followed by a predictable anti-climax... One of the main acts invariably doesn't turn up, the day drags on so long you're too stoned to remember the one band you wanted to see, and it's such a *las* to go to the loo that everyone ends up peeing in water bottles – which then end up being thrown in the air. Woodstock it ain't.

Bitter expats

South Africans don't exactly have a reputation for covering themselves in glory when they're abroad. We're such a cliquey bunch that we inevitably end up in the same pub in Putney, getting trolleyed every weekend or making a nuisance of ourselves at rugby matches all covered in green and gold. But hey, at least we're usually proud enough to stand up and sing *Nkosi S'kelel'* before the game. Even if it is really badly. And the UK or Sydney or Dubai is just a temporary thing anyway, right?

The really problematic South Africans abroad are the bitter expatriates who've emigrated in the last ten or so years. One-eyed racist hard-luck stories, the lot of them.

As opposed to the quiet expat who just heads off overseas and gets on with his new life – and good luck to him – the bitter expat loves nothing more than harping on about how terrible South Africa has become since "they" took over, and how we're all so very irresponsible allowing our children to grow up in such a dreadful and dangerous part of the world. He specialises in relating recent political debacles involving corrupt parliamentarians and crooked cops or reporting the latest drop in the rand or letting you know about his cousin in Boksburg who was hijacked. We're all destined to be murdered in our beds, for sure.

It's the shallowest case of self-justification ever diagnosed. Like the poor loser who had to miss the party and wants to make sure that everyone else had a really bad time. Sure we did, loser, it was just terrible without you.

The way some expats put down South Africa, you would think they will only be satisfied when the country self-destructs in an orgy of political violence and economic woe, so they can say I told you so. In the meantime, they're going to have to be satisfied with the ulcer they've got from thinking about it, and carry on talking as though they've conveniently moved to a utopia – as though the UK has the best weather in the world, as though Australia isn't full of Australians, as though there is actually one hot chick in New Zealand, as though Canada isn't the most boring bloody place in the universe.

Hey, bitter expats, didn't you read the fine print on your exit papers? There's a clause in it that says only *egte* South Africans have the right to whinge about South Africa. When you changed flags you lost that privilege.

You've chosen to move on. Now get over it, you big wet bags.

Bluetooth headsets

It's bad enough when people actually use Bluetooth headsets to take calls. But then some of them keep their sets on their ears when they're done talking. In anticipation of their next call. Which could come at any time. Really. Any time.

Wow, man, you're obviously very important. And you're lame. Take it off, please.

Bono's role in the world

It's not so much that Bono used to be a legend, lead singer of one of the greatest bands in the world, and now he sings songs that make you want to claw your ears off. Because then you'd feel the same about Simon le Bon – and you don't want to punch Simon le Bon in the mouth, do you? Or Robert Smith, for that matter. It's not even that Bono's a self-important poser who says things in interviews that make you want to run screaming into the night as though you're naked and on fire. Because, to be fair, sometimes he says things that make sense. Well, kind of.

It's the fact that his job is to be a rock star, not a politician. But the politicians are even worse at their job than Bono. Next thing Kofi Annan will form a rock group called Midnight Oil-for-Food Programme, and Dubya Bush will roar up the charts with his hit single *I Still Haven't Found The Weapons Of Mass Destruction I Was Looking For.*

Book royalties

It works out at about 45c an hour. That guy on the side of the road with the fake amputated leg – he gets more.

Braai meddlers

Most Saffers know the code of the braai, but there's always one guy who steals the tongs when you're not looking, pokes the coals indiscriminately, pricks the boerie without asking and tries to jump the meat queue. Odds are he'll be the oke shouting at the ref later before heading to Montecasino for an evening of high culture.

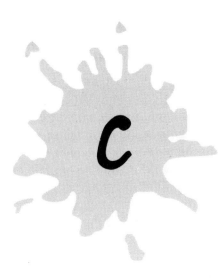

Call centres

You think to yourself – while you're pushing 1 for general enquiries, then selecting 2 for English, then entering your ID number on the telephone keypad followed by hash, then hearing a semi-famous voice say, "You have not entered the correct number of digits; please enter your ID number on the telephone keypad followed by hash", then re-entering your ID number on the telephone keypad followed by hash, then entering the cellphone number from which you were calling followed by hash, as if these people haven't heard of caller ID, they're a telecommunications company for god's sake – that you'd like to speak to a real person. So, at the first opportunity, you push whichever number will get you through to the next available operator. After 25 minutes of trying to decide which hurts your ears more, Kenny G jamming on his alto sax or the semi-famous voice telling you how important your call is, what you feel when you hear, "Hello, Really Big Cellphone Company, this is Shaun, how can I help you?" is joy.

And then, within seconds, you realise that the semi-famous voice was a better option after all. Shaun wants your ID number and your cell number. Again. Because the system didn't pick them up. Because it never does. And Shaun doesn't know why your phone has been cut off. What he does know is how long it'll take to be switched on again: 72 hours. You ask for his supervisor. He cuts you off.

Repeat process.

Get through to Moses. Moses says you haven't paid your account, and will be reconnected 48 hours after paying. He doesn't know why your debit order went through from your account but didn't get to the cellphone people. He also doesn't know why Shaun told you the things he did. You can't hear him properly so you give up.

Then you start weeping like a menopausal woman.

By this point, you realise you've missed two meetings, a civil war and a major sporting final.

Here's the secret: if you'd phoned 1023 to find out about your cellphone problem, you'd have got just as much help. That's because there is only one call centre in South Africa. It's manned by homeless people off the street, who are given headphones and told to say whatever they like. Next time, just phone Britney Spears. You might as well.

Cape Town's rip-off mentality

The fact that so many of us have a take-what-you-can-get-and-run attitude these days should probably come as no surprise. Just look at all our inspiration: Telkom, members of parliament, our banks, professional sportsmen... But Capetonians just seem so much worse than everyone else. This is presumably what happens when enough Poms and Germans to start a world war make a place their regular destination of choice and then gleefully throw around their pounds and euros in between picking up heatstroke on Clifton 4th and rent boys in Green Point. In that sense, Cape Town is, I imagine, kind of like the Western Front circa 1916. Actually, I doubt the war vets could have handled Camps Bay in summer. Freezer-burn crayfish at R9,000 a tail with a side portion of McCains seasonal vegetables (extra), or a bowl of rat-tail gruel in a trench? The trench, good sir. Would rather be shelled than shafted, what! Tally ho!

Car guards

No-one can begrudge the baton-wielding Congolese gentleman who looks after your car at night, because he's actually performing a service. If it wasn't for him, there's a fair to middling chance your car, or large parts of it, would not be there when you returned from dinner. And besides, he's probably a qualified lawyer. But the middle-of-the-day chancers, who arrive just as you've finished parallel parking to tell you they'll look after your car one time, are beyond the pale. If ever the phrase "Thanks for nothing, asshole!" applies, it's as you pull away from some R5-richer clown in a tatty reflective bib who has just directed you out of your three-car-long parking spot right outside the corner café where you've spent a minute buying the paper.

Car-park faffers
Sandton Square is not the easiest place in the world to find parking, so when you get back to your car I would appreciate it greatly if you could kindly vacate your spot in as expeditious a manner as possible. Put the cellphone away, postpone the makeup application until you get home and leave your handbag alone. Just leave it the hell alone. The road rage getting here was bad enough and I don't need any further temptation to get out of my car and beat you about the head with your golden stilettos.

Cellphone cinema etiquette
It is legal to physically assault someone talking on his cellphone in the cinema. Really, it is. What's that? It isn't?! Oh. Well, it should be.

Cellphone ring tones
If you are so inclined, it is possible to download onto your cellphone (and pay for) the sound of a baby crying and use it as your ring tone. The television commercial advertising this deal describes the ring tone as "annoying", a refreshing stab at honesty, though a more accurate description would have been "incredibly, incredibly, incredibly annoying". What is the implication here? That you want to be annoyed every time your phone rings? Or that you want to annoy the people around you every time your phone rings? Or that you just want to attract attention to yourself? Grow up and get the *William Tell Overture* or something. Then TURN DOWN THE VOLUME! You are not the centre of the universe.

Conspiracy theories
Americans have been fretting over who killed JFK since 1963. It's probably the most well-known, convoluted conspiracy theory of all time. Silly

Americans. Why fuss over just one conspiracy when you can have one a day here in South Africa?

A Koeberg nuclear reactor goes down. Incompetence? Human error? Oh no! A conspiracy by anti-democratic forces.

Rape and corruption charges instigated against the deputy president. Dodgy dealings? Character defects? No way! Shadowy elements out to get him.

Widespread cable theft reported throughout the country. Easy targets for criminals? Crime out of control? No, a sabotage plot to cripple the economy!

Newspaper investigations reveal the minister of health to be an obnoxious drunk and a thief. Solid journalism? Information the public needs to know? Not a chance! A loose-cannon newspaper with a subversive agenda.

Sure it is, guys. Sure it is.

Fiona Coyne

She *wishes* she was Anne Robinson. Sorry, sweetheart, you need a razor-sharp tongue, a pervasive air of condescension and a history of alcoholism to follow in her footsteps. Work on it. I suggest you start with the alcoholism.

Creatives

Whoever came up with this term to describe people in arty, design-related jobs probably thought he'd got it pretty much spot on, what with them generally being quite a creative bunch. But he got it wrong. I believe the term he was looking for was "wankers". Besides excluding all the people who actually create things – builders and carpenters and such and such – "creatives" doesn't quite capture that intangible air of self-centred, capricious, shallow, irrational egocentricity that tends to define most art directors, decorators and interior designers. Of course, the more senior these people come, the bigger "creatives" they tend to be, alternating, as they do, between thinking that the world revolves around them and thinking that the world should stop revolving just so they can concentrate for a minute.

Crime

Apparently we don't have a crime problem. So nothing to write about, then. (But see **Inconvenient truths…** and **Charles Nqakula**.)

Crocs

Seldom am I at a loss for words when describing the sheer kakness of something, but…

Hansie Cronje

It's not done to mock the dead. "You can't say that!" is the cry when you pass disparaging comments about the recently departed. "He can't defend himself any more. And what about his good qualities? Why don't you focus on those?"

It's understandable in a way, a kind of personal reputation insurance for when we die – because we wouldn't want people to say nasty things about *us*… And it really is the ultimate example of kicking a guy while he's down. But hey, sometimes dead people deserve it. Take Saddam Hussein, for example.

Deep down, Saddam may have been a sensitive type who liked kittens and sunset strolls, but he also personally executed various members of his extended family and cabinet, had his own countrymen gassed and was directly responsible for starting the Iran/Iraq War and First Gulf War. So it's okay to call him a douche bag now. He deserves it. Even though he can't stand up for himself any more, or send the Iraqi secret police to suspend you from a rotating fan. Which is something they liked to do, apparently.

You know who else deserves it? Yup, Hansie Cronje. But say a nasty word about our very own Captain Controversy and you get the might of the righteous Ray McCauley Born Agains coming down on you, with able assistance from a plethora of holy sportsmen who played alongside him back in the day. "How can you badmouth a man who died so tragically?" they cry. "Let him rest in piece! He was a good Christian!"

Er, no he wasn't.

Cronje was as devious and manipulative as they come. He abused the trust and goodwill of his family, his teammates and opponents, and every cricket supporter in the world. He lied and he cheated. Then he lied some more. This makes him a bad Christian.

But, to many, Cronje has gone to his grave as a great human who "made some personal mistakes". And that's "great human", as in number 11 on SABC 3's all-time list of Great South Africans, as voted by the public in 2004. One spot behind Desmond Tutu. And 39 spots ahead of Francois Pienaar – the honest South African sports captain, who actually won the World Cup. Fair enough, we can't put too much stock in a list that has Winnie Madikizela-Mandela at seven and HF Verwoed at 19, but the point is Cronje's death seemed to galvanise a public forgiveness, inspired by a televised funeral and fickle press who possibly felt a little guilty that they'd called him rude names not too long before. The slate was wiped clean by many. For no real reason

Here was a perfect hero and role model for aspiring youngsters, who did just about everything wrong: he sold out his country and supporters for financial gain; he abused a hallowed position of power; he took criminal advantage of naïve teammates who idolised him; and he lied. A lot. And his devil-made-me-do-it, embrace-the-sinner public wailing should not be enough to cleanse his reputation. Particularly so when the rumours still abound that he didn't come clean at the King Commission – that all sorts of secrets are still hidden under the Cronje bed, along with the dirty money.

Look, he's not quite Saddam, but *gee Hansie 'n kansie*? Not for a leather jacket.

CSI

Jesus, the criminals on *CSI* are hopeless. They're easier to crack than a quail's egg. Either that or those remarkably efficient CSI detectives have some secret interrogation tricks we don't know about.

> HORATIO KANE [TAKING OFF SUNGLASSES]: Why did you kill her?
> HOPELESS CRIMINAL: I didn't do it.
> HORATIO KANE [PUTTING ON SUNGLASSES]: Oh yes… you did.
> HOPELESS CRIMINAL [LOOKING AWAY IN SHAME]: Okay, I confess! It was me! Just stop taking off your sunglasses and putting them back on!

Seriously, have you seen how often he does that?

Cycling attire

If there's one kind of exercise nut with an unbearable sense of smug self-satisfaction, it's a road cyclist. Bloody road cyclists.

Most runners just go out there and get it over with as quickly as possible, and mountain bikers at least head out into the hills and out of your face. But road cyclists like nothing more than to spend an entire Sunday morning hogging single-lane uphills in their sanctimonious little pelotons as drivers go slowly insane behind them while developing baseball-bat-out-of-car-window fantasies. Then, when you accidentally-on-purpose almost run them off the road as you overtake, you might, as you roar into the distance, catch a "Hey watch it! Cyclists have rights too!"

No, buddy, I'm afraid you gave up your rights when you left your house all dressed up like a raver. Everyone else's rights not to be visually offended by you take preference here.

Given the hideous plague of obesity that is sweeping the planet, some credit must be given to people trying to stay in shape. So we'll forgive cyclists their dorky tans and shaved legs. But what is it with the retarded fashions? The shocking psychedelic colours, the tighter-than-tight fits, the sunglasses that closely resemble early '90s Top Sport D'Arcs…

Are these people shameless attention seekers? Has the groin pressure affected their brains? Or are they, perhaps, blind? Presumably not, otherwise they'd almost certainly find slipstreaming tricky. Whatever the reason, someone needs to pass on the message that T-Mobile and Rabobank professional road racers get paid to wear their hideous cycling outfits – which is to say, they don't have a choice. And said messenger might also want to let them know that going to a coffee shop in full cycling kit after spending four hours in the saddle is not on. You don't see marathon runners in their polyshorts pulling in for muffins and espressos, so why do you think it's cool to rock up in your pink Lycra budgie-smugglers?

The DA

It's almost unfair to include the DA here. It's kind of like blaming a sausage dog for not mauling to death the local pit bull. Because about all the sausage dog can do is bark.

But it could at least try to bark at the right things. After a while, when you're yapping away at just about everything under the sun, no-one really cares what it is you're yapping at; they just think of ways to put you down.

Come on, DA! The ANC is practically cleaved in two. Stop taking shit from pissy little upstarts like the ID and the African Christian Democrats (I mean, *really*) and make up some ground here! If you can't show some meaningful, marginally influential opposition right now, you may as well just give up. Go on, throw that sausage dog in among the pigeons.

Divas

The term "diva" used to refer to a female opera singer. Now it also applies to screechy pop stars whose secondary claims to fame may or may not include a history of drug abuse, eating disorders, emotional breakdowns, personal bankruptcy, gross narcissism, failed acting careers and/or the enduring ability to charge inordinately high prices for concert tickets.

The world's most heinous divas, in alphabetical order:

Toni Braxton

Mariah Carey
Celine Dion
Whitney Houston
Barbara Streisand

* Legal disclaimer: we're not saying that all those nasty things over the page apply to all these divas, necessarily. Just to be clear on that, girls. Because we know how you get.

Diving

For so long, diving has been a bane of that pansy sport, soccer. Flamboyant soccer boys like nothing more than falling to the ground like hysterical women if they think they can sneak a penalty from the referee. FIFA could have sorted out the problem years ago by citing players after the game and banning them, but soccer is as much entertainment as sport these days (see **Professional sport**), and FIFA officials are more concerned with policing trademark infringements and involving themselves in city planning than improving the game (see **FIFA**), so we can't be too surprised nothing's been done about it. Still, it's only soccer, so no point in getting too worked up.

But now this devious prima donna tactic is increasingly being adopted by rugby players looking for cheap points or, worse, hoping to get opposition players sent off. It's truly pathetic stuff. The Argentinians, with their girlie long hair and strong soccer background, are prime offenders. Some of those Frenchies, too.

Someone with influence somewhere needs to step in and remind everyone that rugby is a contact sport and, unlike diving, it's not for fairies. For an example to lead by, consider ex-All Black Andy Dalton who, on having his jaw broken in two places in 1986 by Bok thug Burger Geldenhuys during the New Zealand Cavaliers tour of South Africa, had this to say: "No complaints. It's a man's game out there."

Or try the immortal words of Tana Umaga: "It's not Tiddlywinks, ref." Damn right.

Documentaries that last one hour when they should last 15 minutes

Right. We have a cool topic, some grainy footage and a teeny bit of interesting information.

How can we stretch this subject matter over a full hour?

It will be difficult.

But we will try.

Really hard.

Almost annoyingly hard, in fact.

So hard, that every bone in your body will impel you to change channels.

But you won't.

Because you want to see how it ends.

[Ad break]

We have been discussing how to stretch out this cool topic with some grainy footage over a full hour.

We established that it would be difficult but that we would try really hard.

We also established that you will want to change channels but you won't.

Coming up, we will replay the same grainy footage.

Over and over and over.

And tell you how.

We've managed.

To stretch out.

This topic

Over a

Full

H

o

u

r

.

You'd think we would just look up the Dambusters on the net for five minutes and then switch over to Fashion TV. If only it was that easy.

"Domestic"

The meddlesome PC fraternity, who make it their life ambition to suck the vitality from the world around us, have deemed "domestic" the correct modern appellation for someone who cleans your house. So, what, "maid" just suddenly ceases to exist? There's nothing wrong with maid, which isn't derogatory and simply means "a woman employed to do housework". A "domestic" is a suburban incident in the United States involving a man, his wife, a string vest and a couple of bottles of Jack Daniel's.

DSTV reception

You pay a third of your salary a month for a million channels, most of which are bunk, and as soon as a light zephyr starts rustling the trees near your satellite dish or a patter of rain falls, your screen starts pixellating. Then you get angry and try pressing random buttons on your delayed-action DSTV remote, which makes the screen freeze, so you have to reboot the whole frikking thing, and then it won't establish a connection, so you phone the helpline and get the automatic answering system… *For billing information or account queries, press 1. For technical or transmission queries, press 2. For brain aneurisms and the plague, press 3…*

You need a really good mantra just to cope. I go with "SuperSport is the best sports channel in the world, SuperSport is the best sports channel in the world, SuperSport is the best sports channel in the world…" Sometimes it works, sometimes the remote gets it.

Dual-flush cisterns that don't flush properly

It's a noble invention, the dual-flush cistern, with good reason for existence. Water conservation is vital. So I always make a point of using the half flush when I've drained the monster. Hell, sometimes I just leave it there to mellow. For the environment.

The problem is the full flush on these new toilets. Full, my ass. Time was you could drop a small sheep in a toilet and it was guaranteed to go down. And I'm not talking in euphemisms here; you could flush an actual small sheep down the toilet. Sure, that's overkill, but now we've gone to the other extreme.

It's a struggle to dispose of a mere fart nowadays. Sometimes you've got to flush three or four times so your skidmark is just embarrassing

– rather than monumentally embarrassing. Then, if it's a public toilet you're stepping out of, the walk of shame is mortifying. If you've got someone waiting his turn you may as well go back in there and bogwash yourself. Because you *know* he's going to be staring down at that bowl thinking, "God, he flushed four times and it still looks like an Easter bunny was murdered down there. The filthy, filthy pig."

The only explanation I can think of is that new dual-flush toilets are designed and created by women – because women think that going to the lavatory is a 30-second exercise in producing light wind and a lone *bokdrolletjie*. "Dropping the kids off at the pool" has no meaning for them because children possess mass and physical presence, while women actually only flush to get rid of the paper, which is superfluous anyway. Women don't understand that men take the newspaper with them when they head off for a dump not because we like to read in the bathroom, but so we don't get bored. This is a working theory, but I stand by it.

Anyway, try ramming a fillet steak and two bottles of wine down there these days. Not pretty.

E-mail chain letters

People have been complaining about e-mail chain letters for years. You know the ones: guilt-laden sob stories, appalling drippy poems, cutesy puppy pictures, humourless jokes, obvious hoaxes – all with ominous postscripts commanding readers to forward them on or face the consequences. No luck, no love, no penis, no millions from Bill Gates – this is what awaits you if you don't press "Send".

These e-mails have been clogging up our inboxes and filling us with rage since the day the World Wide Web came online, and everyone agrees they're more annoying than a Jehova's Witness making house calls. There are countless websites, magazine articles and even e-mail forwards dedicated to expressing these sentiments.

This begs the question: if everyone complains about them, surely there should be no-one left to send them? Right? So who the fuck keeps doing it?

At last count, there were more of these e-mail chain letters perpetuating their annoying vibes across the internet than there are stars in the galaxy. What is it going to take to stop the cretins of the world from propagating these useless, time-wasting black holes of useless time wasting?

Perhaps a worldwide eugenics programme, specific to eliminating the propensity for e-mail forwarding, would do the trick. Keep the good genes, weed out the retards. It sounds harsh, but desperate times and all.

Just picture a breeding candidate answering questions from a eugenics officer at a future reproduction-screening interview and you'll already start calming down.

"You receive an e-mail that claims your penis will fall off if you do not forward it immediately to everyone on your mailing list. Do you send it on?"

"Er… Yes."

"STUPID! NO BABIES!"

Another screening interview might go like this:

"You receive an e-mail that reads, 'You will be lucky in love if you forward this to 5-10 people, you will be really lucky in love if you forward this to 10-20 people and you will meet your soul mate within a week if you forward it to more than 20 people. Trust me! This is for real!!!' What do you do?"

"Delete it. But only after replying to inform the sender that he is a dick. Then fly kick the sender at the next available opportunity."

"Intelligent. Breeding permissible."

Alas, even this solution has its perils. Would the inevitable inbreeding-related birth defects be worth it? Personally I'd take a cleft palate over a chronic chain-mailer any day of the week. At least you can operate on the one – lobotomies aside.

The English Football Team

Prior to every World and European Cup, the hysterical English press touts its team for success.

Rooney's a genius!
Beckham has the heart!
Rio's the rock!
We can do it!

And after every World and European Cup the same hysterical English press brutally lambasts its team for being a bunch of spineless losers. English press, you are getting it right half the time.

Eskom

In September 2007, Eskom warned South Africans that they were likely to suffer more power failures and shortages the following year. "Winter

2008 is going to be more challenging than winter 2007," said Jacob Maroga, CEO of Eskom. There are, he continued, likely to be worsening failures and shortages in the next eight years, as Eskom's reserve margins decline in that time.

Once again, we, the consumers, have effectively been asked to do Eskom's job by limiting our electricity usage and not putting too much strain on the system. Fine. I am a good citizen; I'm willing to do my bit. You know what, I'll even go beyond the call of duty. For instance, I'll put together the next Eskom press release, if that's okay.

"Important announcement: Eskom has finally decided to come clean and admit that for some time it's been run by a bunch of palookas who can't tell their arses from their elbows. But don't worry about the pebble-bed nuclear reactors. We're almost sure we know what we're doing. Promise!"

Just to repeat that: THE NEXT EIGHT YEARS.

Evaluation forms

Good to know they at least like to make a show of caring, but do we really need to fill in forms with little smiley faces on them everywhere we go? Given what we think of smiley faces and all? (See **Smiley faces**.)

Buy a burger – "How was our service?"

Pass through an airport – "SMS us your comments!"

Check out of hospital – "Tell us how you enjoyed your visit"

Visit a brothel – "How was it for you?"

You can spend more time filling out forms and ticking boxes than actually driving your rental car. And, even worse, just because companies offer this evaluation service they think they have improved already. I've got a crap business with crap service, but here's an evaluation form to make us all feel much better. Who analyses these forms? And do they really go and tell Joanne at the front desk that she's been voted rude bitch of the month three months running?

4th Avenue, Parkhurst

Joburg's café-dining trend centre! So hip, so viby, so… average.

Famous-quotation marketing

Can't afford to pay someone to come up with a great sales idea for your new health spa, restaurant menu or retirement policy? Not to worry. Just get Einstein or Gandhi or a renowned artist or intellectual to help you out. Hit Google, find a nice little quote from a world figure, and you're away.

Here's one by Pablo Picasso: *The purpose of art is washing the dust of daily life off our souls*. Now superimpose this over a photograph of your indoor heated spa pool and you're done. Yes, folks! Picasso had a fantastic seaweed face mask and back rub here; you should really try it, too!

Or, from Khalil Gibran: *Forget not that the earth delights to feel your bare feet and the winds long to play with your hair*. Don't really understand what he's on about? Relax. No need to stress over what it actually means. People don't really care, anyway; it just looks good.

This type of appeal-to-authority persuasion works on suckers all the time, especially if they don't really know what your quote guy was up to. Spanish weirdo who drew cubes and stuff – must have been a visionary. Lebanese-American poet/artist guy – I believe him!

To help you get started with this easy-to-use, highly effective recipe,

just mix these ingredients for your next cheap advertising campaign:
1. obscure, arty photograph that could be anywhere in the world
2. famous quote
3. your address and phone number (website optional).
It can't not work.

Fashionistas

"Fashionista" – a PR gem that effectively describes male bimbos in designer vests and white pants, and brainless women wearing oversized sunglasses at night. A no-brain description du jour. Fashion isn't about trends, people; it's about style.

FIFA

Why does Cape Town have a multibillion-rand sports stadium going up on the Green Point common, as far from Cape Town's soccer-watching communities as geographically possible without being in another province? Because FIFA said so. Never mind that bringing-the-game-to-the-people nonsense; we need the mountain backdrop.

We can't speculate on whether or not there was a bribe involved because FIFA's not afraid to get in the lawyers. Just writing the word "FIFA" is a bit risky, actually, because they have applied for it to be trademark protected, along with the likes of "2010", "World Cup" and "South African". Next, they'll trademark the phrase, "It's all about the money".

Floor crossing

The DA has done very little to mould the political path that South Africa has trod since 1994, but one piece of legislation it ably encouraged into being allows MPs and government councillors to move to another party, along with their original vote. The DA should be as proud of floor crossing as the Yanks are of sponsoring Osama Bin Laden in the '80s.

Floor crossing is costly, lends itself to bribery and corruption, and defies spectacularly the point of democratic elections. In short, it defines perfectly what dishonourable, self-serving, fair-weather scum politicians are. Here's an example: Stan Simmons. In 2005, Simmons crossed from the NNP to form the single-member United Party Of South Africa, one of five new parties that reportedly cost taxpayers R10.5 million at the time. Then, in the 2007 window, he stabbed himself in the back and crossed over to a new one-man party called the National Alliance. What a guy.

Flower sellers in restaurants

Is there anything less romantic than a spotty chick trying to guilt you into buying an exorbitantly priced rose for your date, supposedly in the name of charity? A fart sandwich, perhaps?

Fun-loving Russians

Not since the Angolan bush war has so much Russian been heard in this part of the world. While Russians at home are trying desperately to create a modern, Westernised image of themselves, we are portraying them as jovial proletarian peasants. It's suddenly become trendy to advertise anything remotely Russian with the full fanfare of a traditional wedding, balalaikas at full pitch. Vodka goes without saying. Instead of falling in line with most alcohol advertising that portrays sophisticated modern-lifestyle scenarios, vodka adverts have missed out on about 100 years of history and would have you believe that the Tsar is still hanging out at his palace. Other ads show fun-loving Russkies having endless parties with huskies, babes and alcopops that are hardly likely to impress your average comrade. The accents get played to the fullest, with Boris telling you how cool it is to do crazy shit at -25 degrees. All very well to show the old stereotypes that don't exists anymore, but a bit insensitive when you consider that 25 million Russians are alcoholics. A social system that didn't leave much room for self-development has delivered a harvest of wrecked dreams half the size of the South African population. Dop system? Foetal alcohol syndrome? We've got nothing on the Russians.

"Funny" music on TV shows

Desperate Housewives would be desperate enough as it is, but the X-factor that lifts it into the upper echelons of complete television rubbish is surely the plinky-plonky "funny" music that indicates to viewers when it's time to laugh. Because without the music they might be thinking it's time to go take a dump. Which is, of course, the better option.

The Gautrain

Four years of detours, power failures and midnight explosions had better be worth it. Not to mention the R10 billion-plus price tag.

Gwen Gill's disturbingly likeable reading list

So much about Gwen Gill is terrible. She's the "doyenne of SA celebrity watching", for god's sake. She "brings the glitzy lives of jetsetters, models, politicians and sports personalities to our attention every week", for crying out loud. It's hard to get more painful than that – and yet she manages it with ease by regularly passing style judgment on these selfsame jetsetters, models, politicians and sports personalities. This from a grandmother who looks like a *Lord Of The Rings* extra. Not to be ageist or lookist or anything, but surely this disqualifies her from the job? Surely she is better qualified to be a cricket commentator or car mechanic?

The real problem with Gwen, however, is that her terribleness is fallible. Rather than being one of those caricatures of evil, like Robert Mugabe or Paris Hilton, whose every action and public comment adds further flames to the fire of revulsion surrounding them, Gwen has, at the very least, a killer reading list. A recent listing of her ten favourite books included *The Hitchhiker's Guide To The Galaxy*, *Slaughterhouse*

Five, The World According To Garp, The Spy Who Came In From The Cold and "any top-class world atlas". This really, really pissed me off.

I was expecting (and hoping) it would feature *Hello!* and *heat* magazines as her top two reads ("I can't decide between them!"), *The Da Vinci Code* at three ("It really made me think"), and a vomitous selection of Jilly Cooper, Barbara Cartland and Jackie Collins novels to follow. But no, there's her list complete with Douglas Adams, Kurt Vonnegut, John Irving and John le Carre. Throw in Martin Amis and Frederick Forsyth and it would be *my* list.

Even Gwen's heavy stuff is good. Annie Proulx may be a tough cookie, but *The Shipping News* is proper writing. And *Pride And Prejudice* was her number one. It's not *Day Of The Jackal*, but you can't shake a stick at Jane Austen. As for the top-class world atlas… that was just the topper. Because atlases are cool. They are manly. They are logical and denote exploration and adventure. They have no connection to celebrity junk culture in any form whatsoever. Come on, Gwen. You were kidding, right?

The God Delusion

In the past, most vaguely intelligent people who took the time and effort to consider deep metaphysical questions in a rational manner would have come to the conclusion that religion is, well, a bit of a waste of time. Magic and sorcery and contradictions and whatnot. And we were quite content keeping this knowledge to ourselves, while telling in-jokes and laughing at the masses (after all, we were the "chosen ones" – a-hahaha!).

Then came *The God Delusion*.

Now that Richard Dawkins has unleashed his secular agitprop, primed for mass appeal, every semi-literate bandwagon-jumper out there is touting atheism as the greatest breakthrough of the 21st century, regularly taking out "the good book" to proselytise in parking lots and shopping malls. Don't get me wrong, Dawkins makes a sound argument – how could he not? – and perhaps the time will come to drag humanity out of its mire of intellectual destitution, but these imbeciles are giving all of us teapot atheists (a term coined by Bertrand Russell – do you even know who that is, imbeciles?!) a bad name.

"Going forward"

Contemporary business-speak successor to the phrase "at this moment in time"; effectively a synonym for "um" or "blah blah blah". As in *Going forward, we need to get our ducks in a row and start thinking outside the box in order to boost profit and maximise performance.*

Don't forget, this must be done going forward. Not backward. Or sideways. Or diagonally even. And definitely not sideways and then diagonally. No no: *forward!* Well, thank goodness we cleared that up.

As when a man says "I love you" after sex, "going forward" is a phrase without meaning.

Green guilt

Never before has so much global hype been aimed at one mission: save the planet! Large industrial countries across the world are trying desperately to show how much they care by trading "green credits" with each other to allow them to spew more filth into the air. We don't have to worry about our carbon footprint down here in South Africa, though; we already have the oldest known footprint in the world, discovered in the mud at Langebaan lagoon and carbon dated to 117,000 years ago. Ka-ching! So don't try to tell us about footprints, you First World polluters.

Anyway, what kind of sick joke are they throwing at us, saying we have to regress in our development just to keep the First World nations happy? It's not enough that they've plundered our resources over the years to drive their economies, with no regard for the environment, but now we're not allowed to do the same? For the first time ever, South Africans of all colours and creeds have the opportunity and financial means to buy whatever cars they want. What's that, Lebo? You want a big 4x4 just like the guys who oppressed you had? No, sorry its not good for the planet. How about this mountain bike? Very healthy for you, you know.

And the rest of you, do your bit to save the planet! Stop importing your mussels from New Zealand and sugar snaps from Kenya. And turn off the air-con. And buy energy-efficient bulbs. And quit using so much paper. And boycott supermarkets with open freezers. And insulate your house. And stop flying.

No flying? Aw, you serious?

Handicapped-loo guilt

It's one thing parking in a handicapped spot but parking one in a handicapped loo – now that's special! The problem is sneaking out without anyone busting you. Stand-alone units are particularly troublesome in this regard. If you have the misfortune of exiting at the same time as a woman from the ladies, whatever you do, do *not* make eye contact: man, that disapproving look burns. You can try to hobble off, as though you were temporarily disabled or something, but she generally won't buy that. And don't even think of trying to explain that it was a monster and you needed to hold on to the rail. Chicks will never get it (see **Dual-flush cisterns**).

Heat magazine

Lindsay Lohan is going to star as Paris Hilton in the movie of her life! Why do I know this? Why?

It upsets me that Lindsay Lohan is a movie star. It upsets me that there is going to be a movie about Paris Hilton – which, in all likelihood, brainless teens across the world will flock to watch. It upsets me that Paris Hilton even exists. And it upsets me most of all that I know all about whatever the hell it is she's doing today and who's going to star in the movie about her. Thanks a lot, *heat*.

I was really happy when Paris was locked away. Hurrah for Schadenfreude! Look up that word in the dictionary and there's a picture of Paris getting locked away and me laughing my ass off. But I would be far happier if she hadn't been locked away at all, and had just stayed out of the news headlines* and out of my life every time I walked into an Engen Quikshop to buy a litre of milk.

But no. There I am waiting to pay for my milk and right next to me at the checkout is *heat*, our very own pioneering goss mag, telling me the latest on Paris.

Come on, you ask, is *heat* that bad? The short answer is yes.

For the long answer I had to physically page through a copy. It was a painful, painful exercise. Honest to god, this is the first header I read inside: "Is Brangelina near their sell-by date?" Stab motion to eye. You'd think that says it all – a grammatically dubious speculation (complete with ball-grating couple moniker) about the relationship of two people who really would prefer it if there were fewer photographers camped outside their home – but it doesn't.

Next I was accosted by scary pictures of horror celebrities, such as Pete Doherty, Amy Winehouse and Justin Timberlake – modern pop icons to be proud of. More stabbing.

Then came the mindless headline section to go with thoroughly uninteresting (but presumably recent) paparazzi pics.

"Posh eats in public!" A picture of Victoria Beckham eating a naartjie. Stab, stab.

Now there's Danny K – aaargghh! Stab! Stab! Stab! And various other forms of self-mutilation. And general all-over body pain.

Then, of course, there are the obligatory photos of celebs not looking absolutely perfect – showing a dimple, or a spot, or a vague hint of cellulite. Just so any "normal" girl reading can feel that little bit more insecure about her body-dysmorphic issues and scream at her boyfriend later on, supposedly because he forgot to scrape his plate but actually because she feels a bit fat. Like Britney. (Thanks again, *heat*!)

And just to reassure you, this is all interspersed with bad puns, cheesy photo captions and generally lame editorial to make gossip-mag journos across the world proud. I was skim reading – and my eyes were bleeding – but I noticed at least one use of the term "love rat". That perennial gem. "Ooh, that sounds good!" you can imagine the editorial team saying excitedly in a book meeting. "Just like something *The Sun* would write!"

Alternatively, you can imagine the editorial team having absolutely no self-respect and saying things like, "I want to die, I want to die."

Reading *heat* you can feel the guilt start pumping through your veins. And it isn't pleasurable guilt, as with online gambling or masturbating at work; no, it's the guilt of perpetuating pure rubbish. A guilt that makes you want to bang your head repeatedly against a brick wall, because this is where the world is today.

One last thing: is it just me or do the Ohlsen twins have grotesquely oversized heads?

* *A special congratulatory mention goes to American MSNBC news anchor Mika Brzezinski, who refused to read her station's lead story on the morning of 26 June 2007 when she discovered that it was a report on Paris Hilton getting out jail. She preferred to tear up her script live on international television. Mika, this entry is for you.*

Historical-letter writing

Contrary to the popular belief that history is written by those in power throughout the ages, South African history has its own narrators in the form of the average guy next door. No, you don't need to be a qualified history buff, or even anyone of any importance. Simply send your interpretation of our past to any national newspaper letters page. Here you'll find the truth. From people who were there. Or at least their grandparents were. Maybe.

These facts are now the new versions of what happened in our past, and all those elitist history books written by qualified researchers can be ignored.

"Shaka was a bloody murderer," twittles John Poncy-Poncingford of Constantia. "He slaughtered a million of his own people. Why should we honour him as a hero?"

But Shaka's great great grandnephew, Shadrack Tshabalala, is having none of it: "The apartheid forces driven by capitalist greed and post-colonial, imperialist evil massacred our people through a systematic process of genocide, last seen with Hitler."

Newspaper editors look on in glee as the "race" button is hit (see **Racial obsessing**) and reader comments start flooding in by e-mail, SMS, post and hand-written serviettes. A small story on the news about a little boy on the Cape Flats who loses his lunch money takes on the life or death importance of a national catastrophe.

"Jerome Claasens must be feeling the same sense of loss as we, the oppressed, have suffered under the brutal system of job discrimination. His poverty is directly linked to the poverty inflicted by British settlers when they landed at Algoa bay in 1820 and stole his ancestral farm. We will not be silent until this historical injustice is undone!"

May as well tell the schools to get rid of the history books. After all, they only give boring, stuffy facts – there's no blame or finger pointing. Much more fun to make it somebody's fault! A nice emotive exploration of our past will ensure that our children will continue to bicker long into the future.

Or maybe we could all just give it the fuck up?

Hollywood special-effects self-indulgence

When Stanley Kubrick's *2001: A Space Odyssey* was released in 1968, it was rightly hailed as a vision of cinematic genius. Kubrick had merged history, science and philosophy with unprecedented special effects to mark a defining moment in the history of Hollywood. In particular, the final few minutes of *2001* are as iconic a sequence as there exists on film. They are also a rather large load of cinematic masturbation.

An enormous foetus drifts through space. Mirroring the earth. And drifting. And drifting. And music. Loud music. Dun-dun dun-dun dun-dun dun-dun. And cutting-edge special effects. And SYMBOLISM. And more music. And space. All – in – slow – motion...

It's a little ignoble trivialising this great scene like this, but in the context of modern Hollywood's obsession with special effects, there is a point coming along shortly. Essentially, it is this: *2001* may have been great and all, but its legacy is not. Now every Tom, Dick and Michael Bay thinks he's got licence to go mental with the special effects because this is what people want to see.

Let's be clear, for a moment. We're not talking about small-scale cinematic masturbation here. Directors have been churning out self-indulgent crap since the industry first started. Just think existential French cinema or *Lost In Translation* – standard Cinema Nouveau fare that people watch so they can pretend they're intellectuals.

No, we're talking specifically about directors with large budgets and access to special effects who like to apply Kubrickian licence to their work so they can feel clever and superior while directing a film about aliens taking over the earth or really bad weather. Because what we're getting these days is boatloads of big-screen blockbusting wankery: the Michael Bays and John Woos of the world adding better special effects and more explosions and louder music and slower motion to sidestep the expected elements – such as gravity and common sense – and create something to suit their "vision".

But Michael Bay and John Woo are not Stanley Kubrick, who has other great movies on his CV: *Dr Strangelove* and *Full Metal Jacket*, for example. Their movies aren't exactly ground-breaking treatises on the nature of the human soul, either. Their movies are *Pearl Harbour* and *Face/Off*. Which is like comparing the acting ability of Dame Helen Mirren with the acting ability of a Jack Russell, or your cellphone.

So what we get is doves flying in really slow-motion and multiple viewings of the same explosion and bullets emerging from gun barrels and people leaping through the air as if they've been assisted by wires that have been edited out of the picture. Naturally, it's made worse by the influence of the special-effects teams, who the directors just adore.

"Hey, boss," the FX leader on *Broken Arrow* would have said to John Woo before filming on that giant lemon began, "we've worked out how to crash model helicopters." "Awesome!" Cue five helicopter crashes in the movie. Five! Look, I can handle John Travolta stealing nuclear bombs from a B2 bomber, but five consecutive helicopter crashes? Pushing it.

And now, with CGI, we get squadrons of jet fighters flying between buildings and wolves sliding around ice-covered container ships (in central Manhattan) and cars pulling barrel rolls in the air as they knock limpet bombs off their underside... That last one is special: *Transporter 2*, if you haven't seen it. What a load of utter bollocks.

Someone needs to sit these people down and say, "Quentin, you may think you're a genius, and I'm sure you're surrounded by a whole bevy of stinky brown-nosers telling you just that, but you need to take some of the money you're spending on squibs, fake blood and high-wire flying and invest in an editor."

Besides, you can get away with the ending to *2001: A Space Odyssey* just once. In history. As in one guy can get away with it once. Not various guys once each. And Kubrick was that guy. Sorry, Sam Raimi and Zack Snyder and Gore Verbinski and Roland Emmerich and the Wachowski brothers: your opportunity has been lost. Try something else. Stop with the self-indulgent big-screen masturbation.

Home Affairs

According to Home Affairs director-general and hopeful saviour Mavuso Msimang, it will take five years to turn his "abused" department into a competent, working system. About as long as it takes to get a passport, then.

HR departments

You'd like to think that Human Resource people are on your side. But they are not. They are basically management stooges. Meaning, if they can scrape another cent off your salary, they will, even if you're on minimum wage. "Well no, that would be illegal hahaha" – but you know they would if they could.

Officially HR people are meant to be neutral; facilitators between employer and employee, who can arbitrate and mediate. But "arbitrate and mediate" in their lingo means "screw the employee on behalf of management".

So they say they'll get back to you about your tax query, or that missing leave on your pay slip, or the increase you've been hoping for since 2003, but they never do.

And they offer a sympathetic ear, promising confidentiality, as you express your misgivings about your job and your fool boss, then they recite your conversation, word for word, to your fool boss.

And they insist on affirmative action as though they are moral exemplars even if there are just no candidates, then they hire white junior assistants for themselves before turning down a request for a training programme to grow some AA talent because it's too expensive.

And they use all these nice corporate euphemisms such as "performance management" when they mean "crap all over" and "termination" when the mean "fire". Then they performance manage and terminate someone, where after they have the tactlessness to ask, "So, what will you do next?"

"I don't know. You just told me."

"Have you considered waiting tables?"

And they don't bother with actually doing their job and recruiting a replacement when they've terminated someone because the two people still left in Distribution can probably manage the entire department on their own if they get a R250 raise.

And they don't blink when you work overtime – but forget to give them a sick note and there's termination talk.

Hey, HR people, you know that character Arnold Schwarzenegger played, the Terminator? He didn't go around firing people. He blew shit up. Just a word of warning.

Oh, and they are dicks.

Hummers

What is it with Americans? It's like they intentionally set out to make the rest of the world loathe them. Knee-jerk anti-Americans are such trend-seekers that I usually just want to drown them in money and ketchup, but honestly, Americans, you're outdoing yourselves at the moment.

For an obvious example, what exactly was the post-war occupation plan in Iraq?

"Yeah, let's go liberate Iraq and do such a bad job fixin' the place up that even the people who were personally tortured by Saddam long for the old days."

"Nothin' a cluster bomb can't solve!"

"U-S-A! U-S-A! U-S-A!"

Iraq is one thing, but goddamned Hummers are the next level altogether. They take everything bad about SUVs – which is so, so much – and they just supersize the lot of it.

In case you've ever sat waiting behind a Sandton mommy in her Pajero while she's yakking on her phone, or had a Russian bouncer-type driving right up your backside in an X5, and suspected that most SUV drivers are assholes who don't know how to drive, various auto-industry reports will confirm your suspicions. The majority of SUV drivers, they conclude, are "self-centred and self-absorbed" and "insecure and vain"; they are aggressive behind the wheel, they corner too fast (a cause of many fatal rollovers in the '90s), they don't slow down in bad weather and they don't have due respect for other drivers. Officially, the technical term is "assholes who don't know how to drive".

Now, it's difficult to find any reports on Hummer drivers alone, but I'm guessing they'd conclude that driving a Hummer is the loudest possible way of screaming to the world I HAVE MAJOR EGO ISSUES AND A VERY, VERY SMALL COCK! If there is a louder way, you can bet only an American will be able to come up with it.

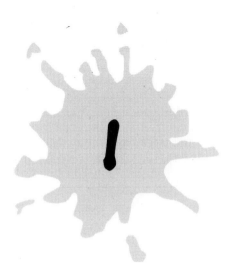

The ID

There's Patricia de Lille, all high and mighty and holier than thou, cracking down on corrupt military deals and racism and whatnot, as she is wont to do – and there are the ID chancers jumping into bed with the ANC after the 2006 Cape Town City Council elections, in the hope that it may just give them an inkling of influence somewhere.

On top of being a spectacular error of judgment, this was hypocritical political opportunism at its best. And rather reminiscent of the NNP. What happened to them, again?

Idiots

There are just so many of them out there...

Idols

The contestants are talentless attention seekers, the judges are self-involved egomaniacs with little or no actual music credibility, and the end product – a CD of vacuous pop music – is an indictment of our times, fit only for idiots (see **Idiots**). And it just won't go away.

Inconvenient truths in An Inconvenient Truth – and other miscellaneous spin

The same week that Al Gore won the 2007 Nobel peace prize for narrating (nice work if you can get it), a UK High Court judge ruled that his record-breaking Oscar-winning documentary *An Inconvenient Truth* had nine significant factual errors in it. Speaking in court, Sir Michael Barton came to the conclusion that the film was a politically partisan, biased analysis of the science of climate change, and included alarmist overstatement and exaggeration. It was, he noted, not merely a science-supported documentary, but rather "a political film".

Hmmm, the former vice-president of the United States making a political film – there could be something to these findings.

Gore was found to have contradicted accepted science by, among other things, blaming Hurricane Katrina and the drying out of Lake Chad directly on climate change; saying the Gulf Stream, which warms the northern Atlantic, was likely to shut down soon, with all kinds of associated meteorological catastrophes; and claiming that the sea could rise by seven metres "in the near future", which is only true if by "the near future" he meant "several thousands of years". Gore's shameless claim that lovable polar bears are drowning in increasing numbers because of longer swims between melting ice floes was also unsubstantiated. Turns out four bears had died in a storm one time.

"Right," you might harrumph disapprovingly if you're liberal and have half a brain, "this is not good. I thought climate change had been proven beyond a shadow of a doubt." (Or, if you're a right-wing Bush lover, you might be going "Gore, you pussy! Woooowoooooowoooo!" and oiling your shotgun.)

But here's the most important aspect of Justice Barton's ruling: he concluded that most of the claims made in the movie were, in fact, backed by widely accepted science, and that the general thrust – that climate change is mainly attributable to man-made emissions of greenhouse gases – was true. Consequently, the film could be shown in British classrooms, with the proviso that it is to be accompanied by guidance notes to balance Gore's "one-sided" views.

So Gore had the weight of scientific evidence on his side – and yet he still lied. That pie-eating bastard!

Why do they do it? Why do they have to spin *everything*?

Sure, it can't ever be forgotten that this is the guy who came second to George W Bush – he is clearly far from perfect – but still, why must he sex up global warming when the reality of the situation is it's bad enough as it is? Just tell the bloody story, man!

Now, because he's been found to have "manipulated the truth" – or however the spin doctors like to spin spin – the climate-change dissidents have the ammo they need to continue arguing. "Global warming? But Gore lied so it must be horsecrap. Only liar we listen to is Dubya. Now let's go shoot stuff!"

Across the world, political spin just keeps on spinning. Never before has humankind been so cynical; never before have we trusted politicians less. And it's infecting more than just politics.

For the British Lions' tour of New Zealand in 2005, coach Clive Woodward brought along Tony Blair's erstwhile spin doctor Alistair Campbell as PR officer. You'd think Campbell, who some people (me) have accurately called "not a nice man", would have had better things to do. Luckily for Sir Clive, though, there were no countries to invade that month, so Campbell could bring his special brand of truth distortion and sensationalism to a nice little rugby tour, hyping up the press over an All Black tackle that injured Brian O'Driscoll, while glossing over the two-month ban Lions lock Danny Grewcock received for biting. And the fact that the Lions were molested three to nothing. Straight out of *The Goebbels Guide To Propaganda And Aryan Supremacy.*

Back home, the SA public has Thabo Mbeki and his Pretoria spokespeople on permanent spin filter. Crime's not a biggie, HIV and AIDS aren't related, the presidential jet is more important than basic service delivery – can we believe *anything* they say?

And the police get in on the act almost every night on the news. Whenever a big drug bust is announced, there is, without fail, one mandatory fact: the "estimated street value" of the drugs, presented as though the cops have just won the lotto. What a great job they're doing! But estimated street value is a load of hogwash; merely an over-inflated guestimate from underpaid cops who just want the public to get off their backs for a while. Where were the drugs going? Who's doing the smuggling? How long has the investigation been going? What does this mean for the affected area? No idea. But the ESV was R100,000! And sea levels are going to rise seven metres in the near future!

A last word on spin, from George W Bush who, being an idiot (see **Idiots**), officially gave the game away at a 2005 discussion on social security: "See, in my line of work you've got to keep repeating things over and over and over again for the truth to sink in, to kind of catapult the propaganda." He was applauded after this line.

In-flight chatterers

"So, do you live in Durban or are you going on holiday?"

"Shut up! Just shut the hell up!"

You may not be an idiot (see **Idiots**), but I suspect you are, so please don't talk to me.

Internuts

Ever noticed how a thread on an online forum or message board can degenerate into a vitriolic slanging match in the blink of a Return key? There you are, having a civilised discussion on the pros and cons of emigration, say, or the merits of going all-in on Jack high, and next thing "ur a a-hole, u got no lif!!" This, according to *Urban Dictionary*, is a phenomenon known as internuts, and its ever-increasing regularity suggests a steady decline in levels of international net etiquette (also known – by nerds – as "netiquette").

Face to face or even on the telephone, people would never dream of speaking to each other like this, and yet the anonymity of the internet allows for a complete abrogation of the niceties of conversational etiquette. The lack of accountability turns average cowardly geeks into the biggest badasses around, spewing emboldened threats and insults at will to whomever deigns to upset them slightly.

These people are idiots (see **Idiots**), and there is only one way to deal with them: stir and antagonise them even more so as to encourage further internuts outbursts and, hopefully, long-term emotional scarring. This has a large measure of satisfaction. But it's a real waste of time.

iPod upgraders

Here's a short list – two things about iPods that are really rather annoying:

1. you can't start a sentence with the word iPod without causing major copy-editing headaches (this originally wasn't a list); and

2. iPod upgraders.

You buy the latest iPod, which can hold your entire music collection 20 times over and then, three months later, they release a new one. Now you no longer own the latest iPod, but it still does the job, so you're happy.

But some people are not happy; they must upgrade to the latest iPod. Over the course of a couple of years, they purchase seven or eight iPods. They can now hold all the music in the world 20 times over. But that is not important. What is important is they have the latest iPod. Idiots. (See **Idiots**.)

Jewellery-shop clerks

"Hi, I would like an engagement ring that I can afford, please."

"Here's a lovely piece. With your salary, you should be able to pay it off in 15 to 20 years. Just remember: the bigger the diamond, the more you love her."

Joburg introductions

"Howzit. Neville Knobend. BMW 330i, 40 grand a month. You guys?"

"Justin Jockstrap. Beemer 530d, 45k."

"Derek Dickwad. Beemer M5, 75k. Just closed a ten-bar deal. Bada-bing."

Once this News Café hierarchy has been established, the next ten minutes are inevitably spent discussing gym memberships and the huge inconvenience of not carrying anything smaller than R200 denominations, as well as tacitly comparing cellphones and watches. Oh, the joys of living in such a friendly, sociable city. At least in Cape Town it's just one question – "What school were you at?" – before you can continue standing around not talking to anyone.

Joost and Amor

SA's very own Posh and Becks. Kinda says it all.

K

Danny K
Looks like a right doos. Could just be me, though.

Keo.co.za
One of South Africa's most popular rugby websites, Keo.co.za should be referred to, whenever possible, as Keocaine – to remind you that it is highly addictive and detrimental to your health.

To be fair, the site is usually first with the latest news, so you can try to overlook the future-imperative tabloid journalism if you're strong-willed. This is tough, though, because you'll think to yourself, why write "They will lose" when describing France's prospects in the World Cup quarterfinal, when you could have written "They should lose" or "They will probably lose" and not look like an idiot the next day when France triumphs and the All Blacks are sent home in ignominy? And you'll think, why write "Poms to paste Wobblies" in a header, then predict England to beat Australia by five in the article, when a five-point margin of victory is anything but a pasting? Then you'll think to yourself, it's because it's much more sensational to make assertive, contentious predictions. Ah, of course. And this will alert you to the fact that your fellow Keo users fall for crap like this all the time and they are, in fact, the real health issue here.

Indeed, the site users who add their (countless) comments to the articles are a mind-blowing mix of juvenile, parochial, narrow-minded, argumentative, racist, frankly embarrassing know-it-alls, who make you ashamed to be a Bok supporter.* Reading their grammar-and-spelling-error-riddled posts is liking staring at the scene of a fatal car crash – it's ghastly, but you just can't help yourself. And suddenly you realise you've lost half an hour of your life forever and you can never have it back. Be strong. Say no to Keocaine.

But then you remember the World Cup and it's all okay again.

The KFC "Friends" campaign

As much as KFC would have liked it, they couldn't actually have "Endorsed by *Friends*" scrawled across the screen in those "Twist it your way" KFC ads with Casey B Dolan and Nick Boraine. But you can tell that's the vibe they're going for – the music, the apartment, the off-the-scale cringe factor.

Knysna

Knysna has won South African town of the year for going on 240 years in a row now. You might think this is a logical impossibility, given that the award has been around for about six months, but that's just how much people love it. Ergo, you might also think it is the best town in South Africa. It is not.

Knysna is a pile of shit. Drive down to the end of Waterfront Drive, onto Thesen Island, and there's a Bose sound-system store. A fucking Bose sound-system store! Towns don't have Bose sound-system stores. Bloody great big cities do. And only some of them.

Just over from the Bose sound-system store is Ile de Pain, probably the best bakery in South Africa. There is always a queue out the door. This is not acceptable for a town. Just not acceptable.

Knysna is no longer a town. It is a monstrosity that has morphed from peaceful lagoon settlement into kitsch designer-holiday borough. While the locals have always been a bit weird and *Deliverance*-y, now the visitors are strange too. They wear orange sunglasses and white three-quarter pants, and they drive BMWs. Goddamned Joburgers.

Not convinced? Take another look at Thesen Island, where you'll also find Thesen Island Development, offering multimillion rand houses for sale with endearing real-estate sales pitches such as "This one is loaded!!!" and "Touches of French Provincial mixed with Cape Cod!" (These are real, by the way, including the exclamation marks.) The second one is particularly eye-catching – you kind of understand what they're trying to say, but it sounds like a menu description in a restaurant run by a family of cretins. Is it a bouillabaisse, perhaps?

Indeed, Thesen Island Development is an interesting concoction. Like a set from *Desperate Housewives* or *The Twilight Zone*, the houses are all different... but they're also strangely the same. Their designs clearly had to meet an exacting set of aesthetic parameters, possibly set by Richie Benaud's tailor. The result is an accumulation of hundreds of wood-panelled pseudo-Hamptons McMansions, thrown together seemingly on the cheap, and all in various shades of beige. Off-white, cream, ivory, pale – it's all very creepy. If you're visiting friends and you take a wrong turn (and the mandatory planned-irregular road layout on a development like this will assist you here), you could drive around for days trying to find your way out. Days!

Weirdness aside, the absolute mind-boggler is that these houses are all built right on top of each other. You pay R6 million for your holiday house so you can reach across and high-five the guy next door as you both take your evening Jacuzzis. Look out to the lagoon and you and your 184 neighbours can appreciate the lovely view together. Word is there are so many houses on Thesen Island, it's now beginning to subside. Land developers – it's not like they're philanthropists.

You used to go to Knysna to get away from it all. Braai, water-ski, chill. Now you go shopping at the Knysna Mall, grab a skinny latte at Vida e Caffé and watch DVDs on your flatscreen (with Bose speakers). Then at night you hit the clubs. What the fuck happened?

Leaf blowers

Cellphones, car-radio remote controls, pedal pushers, automated telephone-answering systems, hip-hop, vegans, religion... The pantheon of enormously kak inventions may be filled to the brim with futile, time-wasting, heinously aggravating creations of man, but one invention towers above all others: the leaf blower, a device that is not only as useless as a cock-flavoured sucker, but is accompanied by sufficient noise to remind everyone within a three-block radius just how useless it is. Beyond a shadow of a doubt, it is the god among kak inventions.

I first encountered leaf blowers several years ago, in New Zealand and then in Canada. These are boring countries, so I figured – mostly while going mental at 9am on Sunday mornings – that the locals just wanted something to keep them busy.

"Nothin' to do, bro. Let's go move some leaves around."

"Choice."

Astoundingly, leaf blowing can entertain your average Kiwi man for anything up to 45 minutes, which gives one ample time to theorise about what could be worse than listening to a small jet engine over the wall when trying to sleep off a hangover. Not much. Leaf blower or a shot of Dave's Insanity Sauce down the Jap's eye? Tough call. But I comforted myself with the knowledge that South Africans could never be motivated to make use of leaf blowers, rationalising that we had

a) more exciting things to do and b) rakes.

That optimism seems to have been unfounded, though, as they are cropping up regularly in this part of the world now. Why, it is hard to say. (Gardeners would tend to make them redundant, surely?) Whatever the reason, it seems a genuine possibility that the intolerable howl of the leaf blower might come to compete with the wail of police sirens as our suburban soundtrack. With that dire thought in mind, this is an appeal to all sane South Africans to disregard any nagging desire to own a leaf blower. If you're really desperate for some wind and noise that has little or no effect other than to irritate and frustrate lots of people, just tune into the Parliament channel.

Libel threats

What do you mean we can't say that?! Everyone knows it's true!

Lift etiquette

Listen carefully. When the lift doors open, let the people who are inside get out first.

Litterers

You think, when you see a stompie chucked out of a car window, that it is a mindless act, that no-one could be that callous and inconsiderate if they just thought for a second about what they were doing. But deep down in that person's soul there is a recognition of what has happened; a tiny voice that acknowledges it. And the voice says, "I am a fucking twat and no-one really likes me."

Listen carefully next time, stompie chuckers.

"Lol"

"Lol" – technically a web-derived acronym for "laughing out loud", but in reality the most overused phrase on the internet and quite possibly the low point in the lexicon of retarded online speak. No-one who uses it is actually laughing, let alone out loud. Instead of containing meaning, it seems to typify the social insecurities of our time – a kind of sycophantic nervous laughter. Essentially, it is a default response for morons who don't know what to say and don't want to offend. If only they knew.

Some examples of its use today:

1. Poker is such a frustrating game.

lol

2. The functional difference between a colon and a semi-colon is great; yet they are both consistently misused.

lol

3. I've had the worst day of my life. My boss fired me, my wife left me, my house burnt down and my kid was run over by a car.

lol

(NB: the last example is probably the only acceptable use of the term lol.)

Madonna

You're nearly 50, Madge. Time to go home, play with the Malawian kids and let the bicep muscles atrophy a bit, don't you think? Maybe get the teeth done, too.

Magazine inserts

Go to shop. See magazine that looks big and bulky and jam-filled with information. Think, ooh, that looks big and bulky and jam-filled with information. Rationalise that this should make magazine good value for money. Buy magazine. Go home. Remove plastic wrapping around magazine and open magazine over rubbish bin. Observe reams and reams of advertising inserts fall into rubbish bin. Note that some inserts are even made out of cardboard. Suffer pang of guilt for multitudes of trees that are hacked down and processed into magazine inserts so that readers can chuck them into bins without reading them. Note that magazine now weighs a third of original weight and appears far less big and bulky and jam-filled with information. Note that magazine, in fact, appears emaciated and decidedly lacking in information. Read magazine in 12 minutes. Note that your last note was pretty much spot-on. Suffer pang of anger for falling for illusion of good value when, in fact, all you were buying was a whole load of horseshit advertising.

Andre Markgraaff

The cockroach of South African rugby. Despite the nuclear explosions that resonate through the sport so regularly, the oke emerges unscathed from the rubble every couple of years to spread about his special breed of divisive pestilence. Where's the Doom when you need it?

Thabo Mbeki

We didn't want to include Thabo. We really didn't. Yes, he's a poseur and not half as clever as he thinks he is – sorry, Thabo, the HIV-not-causing-AIDS theory was a bit of a giveaway – but he also used to have an air of respectability that stood him in good stead next to other world leaders. His "I am an African" speech in 1996 laid the foundations for him to be a worthy successor to Nelson Mandela and, under his presidency, South Africa has prospered, despite the odd controversy here and there.

Lately, though…

For a long time we put up with the crime pooh-poohing and the criminal reaction to the Zimbabwe situation and even the AIDS debacle, but now things have got out of control. It's just not possible to exclude our president from the shitlist when Jacob Zuma – as in *the* Jacob Zuma, the guy who spends a large amount of his time in court defending his honour from rape and corruption accusations or outside court singing about his machine gun – starts sounding more trustworthy than him, and more open to debate and common-sense discussion.

Thabo would have done well to listen to the words of Madiba back in 1997, when he said, "Discussion is the lifeblood of the movement. Do not surround yourself with yes-men." He would have done equally well to have listened to Desmond Tutu in 2004 when he criticised Thabo for doing just that. Instead, Thabo responded by saying that the Arch had never been an ANC member. Very mature. Perhaps one of Thabo's yes-men suggested that response.

The situation has only got worse since. The yes-men (and -women) are still in abundance, and in return for their faithful allegiance they appear to get presidential protection whenever they find themselves in a spot of bother. Never mind the repeated calls for truth and accountability on these issues, or the accusations of cronyism; how about just one believable comment on the Manto or Selebi shams? Or a straight-down-the-line explanation of the demise of the no-men in government: the Vusi Pikolis and Nozizwe Madlala-Routledges? Rather than the Shane Warne rippers or incriminating silences that we are left to deal with.

It seems that our president has been in power long enough that all he hears is what he tells people to say. Read about the phone-tapping, the following of MPs, the harassment of political opponents, and the use of substantial state resources to investigate and potentially prosecute senior journalists on minor charges because of alleged "agendas", and suddenly the leadership styles of Stalin and Mugabe come to mind… Little wonder Thabo isn't too keen on resolving the Zim situation. And little wonder JZ rolled him over at Polokwane.

Minibus taxis

If a wacky scientist type like Christopher Lloyd in *Back To The Future* were to invent a device that measures aggravation and patent it in South Africa, he might be inspired to call it a kakometer. Taking this kakometer into the streets of our towns and cities and pointing it at passing people and objects, he could then have a fun time plotting what it is that generates the least and most aggravation.

Ah, a scandal-mongering *Daily Sun* poster: *Passing Irritation*

And over there, a band of car guards: *Genuine Displeasure*

Is that Danny K I see? *Annoyance Levels Rising!*

But then, with an unnecessary toot of its horn, a minibus taxi pulls up: *Insta-Rage! Warning, Warning! Approaching Ludicrous Aggravation Levels!*

If there is one thing that genuinely unites all South Africans – beyond anything Madiba or a World Cup victory or Chappies bubblegum could ever pull off – it's our hatred of minibus taxis. This is directly related to the guy behind the wheel. Whether he's cutting off other cars, driving in the emergency lane, running red lights or shouting at his passengers for no reason, your average minibus-taxi driver knows his way to the top of the kakometer rating. For good measure, he's not averse to the odd roadside murder.

Combine the power intoxication of a roid-rage bouncer, the incompetence of a Telkom service technician and the sexual morals of Gary Glitter, then add a bit of pure evil, and you've got him. Bob Mugabe would have been a minibus-taxi driver if he hadn't gone into election rigging and economy destruction.

Motorcades

In this thing we call a democracy, we elect a government of the people, by the people, for the people (or whatever order those prepositions are meant to come in) to run the joint. You know, so we don't have to repair our own potholes or draft our own floor-crossing legislation. The beauty of electing this kind of government is that its members are just like us, so they know exactly what our frustrations and needs are.

Ya… actually it doesn't look like they got that memo.

When one of these important men of the people decides to go for a spin, it takes a minimum of five cars to get him anywhere – Black GTIs and X5s with tinted windows and flashing blue lights, book-ended by low-slung traffic-department Beemers. To install their sirens, these cars have had to have gears one to three removed, which is why they can't sit around in traffic like us common folk who only have to get to work and drive the economy. We can wait, obviously, while the radiator boils over and the air-con gas runs out and that radio DJ – you know the one – tries his best to get you in a bad mood.

If you're travelling in KwaZulu-Natal, look out! Because, by all accounts, the motorcade drivers in that part of the world are particularly fast and particularly prone to causing five-car pile-ups when an MP's running late for a funeral or wants to get home in time to catch the beginning of *Egoli*. And if you see, and happen to film, the premier's motorcade speeding and driving recklessly, that's doubly dangerous because it makes you a racist, according to transport MEC Bheki Cele. Well, that's what he called the guy who filmed S'bu Ndebele's convoy doing 160km/h while straddling lanes.

At trying times like these, the wise words of the minister of transport Jeff Radebe are worth recalling. In December 2006, Radebe spoke at an event in Cullinan in Gauteng, telling the crowd that "75 per cent of motor accidents were the result of speeding" – whereafter his convoy raced back to Pretoria at speeds well in excess of 150km/h. Perhaps Jeff thinks VIP stands for Very Ironic Person.

But even better than these single-convoy inconveniences is when our hugely important ministers return to Parliament in a succession of motorcades after a holiday noticeably longer than the 15-day minimum outlined in the Basic Conditions of Employment Act. Roads are closed and snipers sit in trees. Gridlock becomes complete standstill. Then they have a 21-gun salute and a banquet. Of course.

Motoring shows that aren't Top Gear

On a recent episode of *Top Gear Xtra*, they shot a rocket with a car attached to it into the air. Admittedly, it didn't all go to plan, and the whole thing veered off course and crashed back down to earth from an altitude of several hundred metres. But that in itself was just cool. Plus, it was a rocket. With a car attached to it. How are you supposed to beat that?

I don't have the answer – and the other car shows certainly don't, either.

Name changes

Is it Pretoria or is it Tshwane? Anyone? Anyone? Because I really don't know. To be honest, I still haven't worked out which one is Polokwane, and what exactly are they talking about when they say Ekhuruleni? Makhoda, Makopane, Bela-Bela? Don't have a clue.

This name-changing business is a real stinker, isn't it? Why couldn't those apartheid fools name things after flowers and geographical features and stuff? Now we've had to go and shell out R250,000 to change DF Malan Drive to Beyers Naude Drive. And that's for one road only. Then there are the 180 or so proposed street-name changes in Durban. Or is that eThekwini? And another 40-odd in Cape Town. It's still Cape Town, right? Man, I'm going to get so lost.

Just one request: please can we keep South Africa as South Africa? It's part of Africa, it's on the southern end, you can't really read much politics into that – so it kinda makes sense. That would be great. Thanks.

National heroes

In most countries in the world you tend to have to be good at something and excel beyond the norm to achieve greatness. This usually takes a Lifetime Of Unwavering Dedication to a great cause or the Gift Of Insight into a clever business opportunity. Genuine Talent as an entertainer is also an option. Not so in our fantastic land of opportunity, though. Here we can become instant heroes for doing Not Much Really.

So, along with the hundreds of loyalty and rewards cards now available, we offer the average South African a set of tasks which, once achieved, can be redeemed for a fitting National Hero title.

1. Celebrity Status (Bronze): appear at least twice on magazine social pages or have Gwen Gill mention your attire in the *Sunday Times*.
2. Icon Status (Silver): anyone who has a fanbase in his or her local neighbourhood is in with a shot here. An appearance on *Top Billing* with your spouse, kids and dog will help.
3. Legend Status (Gold): five years of doing something vaguely entertaining will do. This doesn't necessarily have to be all good. Drug dealing, gangsterism and general notorious behaviour are acceptable, as the clueless general public finds anyone in the news attractive – good or bad. Just make the occasional headline and you're a winner. Are you that cash-in-transit hijacker who's bribed his way out of prison a dozen times? A sad musician who never knew when to stop? Acted in an SABC soapie? This one's for you.
4. President Status (Platinum): appear in court over a period of not less than eight years on serious charges. Have work colleagues who are in jail. At least five different conspiracy theories involving you should be doing the rounds. Any immoral or anti-establishment gestures such as rape, indecent assault or general intolerance is welcome. As a bonus, you will also have the opportunity to bestow Gold status on ten of your closest friends, bodyguards included.

Note: President Status forms part of our affirmative-action policy. Please check your previously disadvantaged credentials before applying.

Charles Nqakula

February 2008

Dear Minister Of Safety And Security

We know how dedicated you are to keeping up to date on the impact of crime in South Africa, so we thought we should pass on to you the recently released findings of the Ibrahim Index Of African Governance. (You have possibly received these results already, but we suspect you may have thrown them out, thinking they were junk mail.)

Wouldn't you know it, it turns out that South Africa does, in fact, have a crime problem. As of 2005, we were third-worst on a safety-and-security rating of 48 African states, behind only Sudan and Burundi, which were both technically war zones. Congo, Nigeria and Zimbabwe were all safer than South Africa. Even Somalia, with hardly any formal governance to speak of, had an edge over us.

Sorry to break the news to you like this, sir, because we know how absolutely devastated you must be to hear it – not to mention a little embarrassed about your past behaviour when discussing the topic. Don't worry; we all make mistakes! Guess you should listen to the people you work for sometimes, even the white ones – especially considering that the situation is far worse for black people living in townships.

Anyway, we wanted you to know that we have decided against taking your advice. Rather than leaving South Africa, as you suggested, we're going to stay on and just keep whingeing about crime until someone does something about it. Hey, it's our constitutional right – just as its your constitutional duty to protect the citizens of this country.

Sincerely
A couple of whingeing South Africans

PS Let us know if you'd like a free copy of this book.
PPS Sort your shit out.

Blade Nzimande

The general secretary of the South African Communist Party – real name Bonginkosi Nzimande – should possibly have thought out his moniker a little better. Because Blade is a little bit nasty. It rather evokes the thought of knives and stabbing and criminality. Or Wesley Snipes blowing up vampires. Either way, it doesn't scream trust and goodwill. And it doesn't help when all sorts of allegations arise, as they do, against him personally or the SACP or his comrades Zwelinzima Vavi and Jacob Zuma. Everyone's just thinking Blade equals nasty. Then, when he insinuates that all these allegations are counter-revolutionary plots against the SACP and Cosatu and the JZ brigade – well, we're still just thinking nasty.

I suggest a moniker change. How about Nice Nzimande? That's nice.

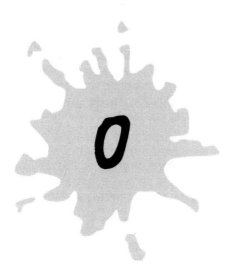

Offensively loud television advertising

"Oh, guys, I'm having yet another problem dealing with McDreamy."

"No problem, Meredith, we're used to it by now. What's up?"

"Well, I can't work out if it's morally acceptable to go out with a guy with such perfect bouffant hair."

"Uh-oh, looks like we'll have to deal with this dilemma after the ad break."

Du-dudu-du-du-du-du.

HARNESS THE POWER OF THE NEW HTC ADVANCED CELLPHONE, WITH BLUETOOTH, MICROSOFT WINDOWS, SATELLITE TRACKING AND PARTICLE ACCELERATOR! THIS AD IS SO LOUD YOU CAN HEAR IT ON OTHER CHANNELS!

Okay, what the hell? When did it become legal and acceptable to assault our auditory senses so brutally and shamelessly?

If you've ever wondered why people down the road can hear what television advertisements you're watching, it's due to an audio-recording effect called extreme dynamic compression. Devious ad makers compress the difference between loud and soft sounds, then they boost it all so that the average sound levels of a commercial are far higher than the average levels of your standard TV show. Those fuckers.

This is cynical marketing at its worst. The logic is: if it's louder, stupid people are more likely to want to buy it. They are counting on your thought process being something along the lines of, "Hmm, the volume has suddenly become insanely loud; I must take note of what they are trying to sell me and go buy it." No, advertisers, you are wrong. You are simply alienating your potential customers, who get really annoyed at HTC for blowing out their eardrums and calling them "fellow sentients", and swear to Odin they will never ever own an HTC product.

PVRs and DVD players have never been more desirable.

And anyway, who came up with that HTC campaign? Whether on full volume or mute, those ads are as annoying as Sarah Jessica Parker doing Garnier commercials. How can the word "avocado" be so aggravating? Ask SJP! And can I just say, *The Family Stone* – what the hell was that all about? What a lame movie – even with Rachel McAdams and Luke Wilson, usually sure-fire winners. Only Sarah Jessica Parker could have ruined it. Hang on a moment. On second thoughts, maybe it was Diane Keaton. Yeah, it was her. She ruins everything.

... on main

Bored with just having a house number? Then get on something. Own the whole street by being *on* it. If you live at 24 Arcadia Street, become 24-on-Arcadia – it's sooo much cooler. But why stop there? How about going one step further and being 24-there-down-by-Arcadia or even 24-loving-it-here-at-Arcadia. Take pride in your place of residence, man. So what if it's only a one-bedroom ground-floor flat in a semi-industrial area. It's not stopping anyone else.

OR Tambo International Airport

Most airports are terrible – that seems to be a sad fact of modern air travel – but OR Tambo just excels in the terrible department. Departures is generally survivable; all travellers have to worry about are unhelpful information-desk personnel, shambolic queues and brainless check-in attendants. But Arrivals, particularly International Arrivals, is a sweat-through-your-pants nightmare. Surly sourpuss immigration officials precede a half-hour wait for your luggage, which, in all likelihood, will have been broken open and pilfered from (if you're lucky, you'll be involved in a shoe exchange), whereafter another surly reception, this time from a customs officer, segues nicely into a malaise of touting taxi drivers and con-men baggage handlers, before you finally force yourself out into the mayhem of traffic outside. If the condor of doom is looking down on you, you will then be followed home and robbed at gunpoint by a criminal syndicate that operates with impunity and probably with the collaboration of surly customs officers…

For all the controversy about renaming the airport, Oliver Tambo would probably not have wanted his name attached to it simply because it is now being associated with incompetence, corruption and general kakness. And this is the first impression of the country for countless visitors. 2010 should be a blast!

Other people
They really are terrible. And they smell.

Oversensitive religious groups
If you're so sure in your convictions – so sure that a moment's utterance by someone you've never met or even heard of compels you to damn him to eternal hellfire – then surely the knowledge that the foul-mouthed heathen in question is going to spend the rest of eternity listening to Helmut Lotti records on repeat while drinking cold coffee amid the fire and brimstone of hell should get you by? I mean, come on! Do you think Jesus/Buddha/Vishnu/The Flying Spaghetti Monster – or the other one we're not allowed to mention (irony alert!) – really needs your extra vitriol to convince him that some Scandinavian guy who doodles cartoons deserves to be hopping about going "Ooh, it burns!" for the rest of time, or that homosexuals are abominations?

Can you imagine your god, up on high, stroking his chin in his infinite wisdom and looking down on the world thinking, "Hmmm, I wasn't too sure whether old Gûdmar should be damned or not, but seeing as Tariq in Lahore is burning a Danish flag, well, that's convinced me." No? Me neither. So, put down the lighter and step away from the petrol can, Tariq. And you, American Family Association, quit giving the gays a hard time and maybe focus on paedophilia in the church and inbreeding and stuff.

"Pant" as a fashion term

Why is it that you can go into Woolworths and buy what's described on the label as a "three-quarter pant"? Why? Why is this? How did a Kaapie butchering of the English language become acceptable fashion speak? It's "pants"!

For correct usage of the term "pant" as an item of clothing, various colourful local terms, such as "naai", "bru" and "kak", need to be deployed. As in, *Naai, bru, I kakked in my pant!*

The same goes for brief, jean, short and trouser.

Paris's parents – and parents in general, for that matter

The obvious question is, why does Paris Hilton not have an entry of her own? She does, after all, come closest to defining the kakness of our times. She is *heat* magazine distilled, if you like. The risk of a stand-alone Paris entry, however, was that it would devolve into a 30,000-word monologue of extreme loathing, limiting space for other entries. That would be unfair on everything else that is kak. And it would take us all to a Very Bad Place (as opposed to the cheerful destination at which we find ourselves when discussing Manto Tshabalala-Msimang, Telkom and the like). But there's a reason Paris exists: blame it on her parents, Rick and Kathy Hilton – and not just in a two-people-had-sex cause-and-effect sense.

As *Spectator* columnist Taki put it, while commenting on how "rubbish" society has become: "With [Paris], it was go from the very minute her white-trash parents began to exhibit her in New York clubs."

And here's Jerry Oppenheimer, author of *House Of Hilton* (and presumed masochist), on Paris's infamous sex video: "Behind the scenes her parents were not opposed to it because that totally launched her."

They were happy, then, to exhibit their daughter before she was launched – by a video of her having sex. If modern parents are the disgrace of contemporary society, then Rick and Kathy are their guiding lights.

On that note there are now, broadly speaking, two types of parents out there. The first goes in for the PC-driven new-age bullshit that claims we should treat five-year-olds like little adults, even though they haven't yet developed the mental faculties to process the world in an adult way. Hence, we must rationalise with them instead of spanking them and allow them the freedom to do as they wish – even if that entails running screaming up and down Woolworths aisles while other (proper adult) shoppers go insane, before the chocolate-induced sugar rush crashes and it all ends in tears. Balance this with completely antithetical notions such as scrapping grades so as not to hurt the little ones' feelings when they don't do so well in class and spoiling them rotten, and their kids grow up thoroughly unprepared for the harsh realities of the world, developing into the offensive, degenerate yobs we encounter every day (see **Teenagers**).

The alternative parenting option adheres to the abandon-baby-in-the-longdrop school of thought. These parents appear in court regularly on domestic-violence and indecent-assault charges, and their kids, if they survive infancy, form the backbone of our criminal underworld. There are complex socio-economic explanations for these parents – destitute backgrounds, spirals of violence, etc – and, in a philosophical sense, you might say they are one side of the balance of humanity. Kind of inevitable. Unfortunately, Rick and Kathy Hilton are not parents of this type. If they were, Paris might be locked up in a Californian penitentiary or coming down off a crack high somewhere… Er, hang on.

Pedestrians

Look left, look right and look left again – didn't we all get taught this at school? No? Oh. Well, that would explain why pedestrians form around 40 per cent of the estimated 12,000 annual road-related deaths in South

Africa. That is some serious road bowling going on. Seems the standard MO is to go out, get merry, then walk home (in non-reflective gear, naturally) along the side of a freeway, while cars whizz by at 150km/h. Unsurprisingly, this method is particularly popular over the holidays.

You're probably familiar with the concept of driving happily along when up pops a guy out of nowhere on the road in front of you. He could be the lost drunk who couldn't believe how wide the pavement had just become. Or the "attitude" jaywalker who thinks it's his democratic right to stroll where he wishes. Or he may be one of a flock of highway-crossers who are banking on the odds being in their favour; like a migratory herd of wildebeest swarming across a crocodile-infested river, each one's hoping he won't get taken.

It's time our esteemed minister of transport, Jeff Radebe, came up with some creative ways to address the issue and get that left-right-left message out there. Or to suggest the use of pedestrian bridges. Along with the endless "Don't Drink And Drive" and "Speed Kills" campaigns targeting drivers, he might consider adding "Don't Drink And Walk" and "Speed The Hell Up When Crossing The Road" campaigns. Thanks, Jeff.

Personal computers

```
This computer has performed an illegal operation
[code: 0X0X290472740]
```

Oh. Thanks for that. I'll just look up that error code in my computer nerd book then, shall I? Before realising that I've possibly just lost four years worth of documents, e-mail, pictures and music. Then I'll go deal with a socially incompetent computer freak at the local IT shop who will nonchalantly tell me "hard drives sometimes fail, man" before glibly charging me a grand for a new one, with little or no deference to the fact that thousands of hours of my personal sweat, emotion and toil have simply disappeared into the computer ether.

"You should get an external drive and back up regularly, man."

"You should shower and try making eye contact, computer nerd."

Whether it's an all-destroying blue screen of death, an unrecognised USB device, an unresponsive printer or – that classic *Fuuuuuck!* moment – a fatal error that crashes your running programs and loses all unsaved information, the cold, cruel computer world just does not have enough respect for the human condition.

Personalised plates

Why go to all the effort and expense of having your number plate registered as HOT STUFF or 1 FLY GUY when you could just write UP MY OWN ARSE! in capitals on your rear windscreen in lipstick? Hey, I'll do it for you if you want.

The Philips Bodygroom body hair trimmer

Have you heard the news? South African women cannot abide men with body hair. Yes, it's true, I'm afraid. If you've got a hirsute chest or fluff on your belly, you are *so* out of the running in the female department. Sorry, buddy, no more sex for you. No more chatting up chicks. No more even looking at women, actually. Just go home and prepare yourself for a future of crying yourself to sleep. Alone.

And god forbid you've got strays sprouting on your neck or errant hairs on your shoulders or – shudder! – your back. You may as well just set up the noose in your garage…

But wait! Don't despair just yet! Maybe there's a solution to the problem. After all, the 2007 survey that produced this definitive conclusion was brought to us by the makers of the Philips Bodygroom shaver and trimmer. In fact, it was called the Philips Bodygroom Survey…

Can you see where they're going with this?

Call me a sceptic, but something tells me the odds of the Philips Bodygroom Survey throwing up a conclusion that the majority of women just *live* for body hair on men are lower than those of Manto Tshabalala-Msimang being wind-pollinated by an AIDS orphan. And yet the news was published – in national newspapers, no less – as definitive scientific analysis. This from Philips: "A group of women were also interviewed, and we found out that only 12% of South African women are attracted to men with body hair. So the hairy men really stand no chance at all."

Excuse me? So we're not allowed to have any body hair whatsoever? After several centuries of putting the hair into hairyback, virile Afrikaner men everywhere – many of them with wives and girlfriends – will no doubt be shocked at this revelation. Not to mention every other guy with a nipple swirl or a snail trail.

And as for the "group of women" – I'm open to correction, but I'm guessing it was made up of eight or nine Philips employees. Quite possibly not all women. ("Look, Barry, just *imagine* you're a woman –

would you want your man to have hair or not?") They will have added the lone dissenting voice – in all likelihood a hideous beast from Accounts (see **Accounts**) – "to give it some credibility". In fact, scratch my doubts; considering the statistics from this survey closely match those from a 2006 research conducted by Philips in the UK, this is clearly what happened.

Come now, Philips. It's not that your product is totally crap. Or an indictment of our metrosexual times. Of course not. But how shameless do you have to be? We may be a gullible bunch of suckers out here – especially the metros – but you have to draw the line somewhere. So I'm making a stand right here.

Say no to manipulative marketing!

Say no to the Philips Bodygroom until they renounce their survey and call it like it is.

Philips, I suggest this approach: "Want to shave your balls? Philips Bodygroom is the way." I'd buy it then.

And to demonstrate just how manipulative the "survey" was, it concluded that, as far as appearances go, "Ryk Neethling is in. Ferdinand Rabie is out." Because of the hair, obviously. Not because the one is a record-breaking Olympic swimming champion with model good looks and the body of a Greek god, while the other is a shifty-looking opportunist who made his name shitting in a garden.

"Please revert"

Instead of asking nicely for a reply, it has become acceptable for modern communicators to append "please revert" to the end of their e-mails. Revert to what, asshole? The happy person I was before I received this nonsensical request with its unfriendly little imperative attitude? That "please" is fooling no-one. How about "I would be grateful if you let me know, thanks, and may I shine your shoes next time I see you"? (NB: "revert" does not mean reply, unless you're in the USA. Are you in the USA? Didn't think so.)

Political apathy

"The situation is terrible. But hey, don't expect me to do anything about it…" Is this an overheard remark from Boutros Boutros-Ghali to a UN delegate about the mass killings in Rwanda in 1994? Or is it George W

Bush telling reporters what he thinks of the Darfur crisis in Sudan? Thabo Mbeki discussing the socio-economic meltdown of Zimbabwe? Ban Ki-moon on Myanmar? Maybe it's a comment referring to genocide in Cambodia or the Congo or the Balkans?

Actually, it's none of the above. It's me addressing my girlfriend as I take a last look at the overflowing garbage bin and head up to bed. If only the leaders of the world set a better example! Then I wouldn't wake up in the morning to be greeted by seagulls in my kitchen. This is a metaphor, politicians. Use it.

Political correctness

Just not really my thing. Bet you didn't see that coming.

Posh's sunglasses

Inordinately large sunglasses are worn by the world's bimbo elite: Beckham, Hilton, Richie et al. As such, they are a calling card of mindlessness. This should serve as motivation enough for other people not to wear them. However, if additional discouragement is required, it has been proven that they are a driving hazard. Honestly. So next time you see a woman wearing saucers on her face, you are fully justified in removing them, flinging them to the floor and jumping up and down on them like Ben Stiller and Owen Wilson in the computer scene in *Zoolander*. Driver safety should never be taken lightly.

Preadolescent sluttiness

Sex is everywhere. In films, in books, in magazines, in advertising, in music videos, on billboards, on our clothes, on our kids' clothes…

On our kids' clothes?

How has it become socially acceptable to dress up five-year-olds in tank tops that say "So many boys, so little time!" or "Eye candy!" on the front? Never mind the stilettos, makeup and padded bras. Say what you want about our nation of promiscuous teenagers and Grade Eight "rainbow" parties, but I don't think it's unreasonable to draw the line at children under the age of, say, ten. Here's the working rule, mom: if she can't spell "paedophile", she shouldn't be dressed up like a harlot. Okay? Okay.

Professional sport

Consider all that is bad about the English Premier League, the world's most watched sporting league: the offensive fans; the revolting on-field behaviour of players; the revolting off-field behaviour of players; the high ticket prices; the insane salaries that see spectator money effectively funding strip-club booze-ups and WAG shopping sprees; the celeb culture that sees players more interested in appearing in magazine fashion shoots and talking about their cars than playing the game; the excess of fixtures; the erosion of the concept of loyalty; the monopolies of the big clubs; the incessant branding of the game; the evolution of sport into entertainment and effectively into business; the vanity; the greed; the steady erosion of all that is "sporting" about football.

All sport is heading in this direction, and it's absolutely tragic.

The Proteas' propensity for choking

The South African one-day cricket team is, for want of a better analogy, the Tim Henman of cricket. We have an attractive playing style, we get crowds totally psyched up and we look great in the early running – then, when the going gets tough, we choke like Jabba the Hutt.

Since the late '90s, the Proteas have consistently been the first- or second-rated ODI team in the world; yet we have just one major ODI tournament victory to our credit: the 1998 ICC Champions Trophy. Remember that? Me neither. Besides that, we haven't even got to a final, being regularly derailed by the likes of Bangladesh, India and the West Indies, teams we beat like red-headed stepchildren when we play them in arbitrary series with nothing on the line.

Despite consistent claims to the contrary from a string of captains and coaches, there is no point in denying our choker tag any longer. Let's just embrace the fact that we have absolutely no BMT* and acknowledge that Okkert Brits has for years been the team's secret psychology consultant, using all the skills he learnt while no-heighting at various Olympic Games and IAAF World Championships despite being one of the greatest pole vaulters in history. Big up to Wayne Ferreira, too, who sometimes assists.

When you think of our cricketers' history of choking in major tournaments, you just have to thank god for the All Blacks.

* *That's short for Big Match Temperament, in case any of the cricketers are reading this.*

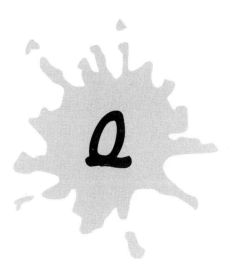

Queues

The last orderly queue in South Africa was during the 1994 general elections. Since then, mayhem.

Quiet diplomacy

Also known as "quiet negligence" or "ineffective diplomacy". Or "wrong".

Quikshops – and other petrol-station mini-markets

There can't have been a more creative response to an unprofitable business then the glut of mini-supermarkets that are opening up at every filling station across the country. The piddly mark-up station owners are allowed to charge on the sale of their petrol was never going to get Hennie de Beer at the Nylstroom BP properly rich. So what started as a boerewors-roll stand run by his wife over the Easter weekend soon led to a fully stocked caravan next to the pumps – and then everyone else started catching on.

While Shell and BP introduced their Select and Express shops, Engen came up with the Quikshop. The alternative spelling is possibly to indicate that the only thing quick about petrol-station stores was the speed at which they sprang up around the country – because you sure can't rely on anything happening quickly once you're inside. They're great if you've forgotten the milk on the way home or are having a hypoglycaemic attack in the middle of nowhere, but there's a price you have to pay. Besides the ridiculous mark-up, that is.

The staff at these new hybrids fall somewhere between being petrol attendants and being supermarket cashiers; they haven't decided which yet. So instead of coming right to you to assist in the aisle, or being stationed and ready to go behind the till, they're kind of arbing around in no-man's land. At any given time, you might find four shop assistants secure behind their bulletproof-glass enclosures, but don't think they're all going to be helping customers. There's Unati packing cigarettes in slow motion; there's Florence talking to a petrol attendant at 500 decibels; there's Thembi with her back to you, flipping through the latest Beare's furniture catalogue; and here's Patience, the only one actually serving, trying without much enthusiasm to scan your Aero for the tenth time. While your chocolate melts in her hands, a growing number of impatient customers – who all struggle with the concept of queueing anyway (see **Queues**) – start edging around you, possibly in the hope that you'll just give up and leave, or pleading with their eyes at the two remaining empty cashiers. When Patience finally cracks that scanning code, she stares at you blankly, presumably attempting to telepathically convey the amount you owe. Bless you, Patience. At least you actually served me.

Quotas

If you don't follow the world golf rankings, you may be surprised to know that in mid 2007 South Africa had seven players in the top 50, and four in the top 20 – a considerable achievement. Now that you know this, chances are you're thinking, "Wow, that's pretty awesome. Go, South African golfers! Hang on, isn't there a sports board whose job it is to stuff this up?" That's what I thought, anyway.

But golf is not a team sport, so any SA golfer can play on the international circuits if he's good enough; no need to worry about quota allowances and governmental interference. On the other hand, when it comes to rugby, cricket, the Olympics – well, no such luck.

Two days before the Rugby World Cup final, Butana Khompela, chairman of the Parliamentary Committee On Sport, had this to say about Springbok coach Jake White: "If he goes today, South African rugby will be better off." Observing that White had "invited trouble" by meddling in politics when he made comments about the difficulties of having to accommodate quota selections, Khompela also said, "I've been saying for a long time that because of the passionate hate Jake White has, I think [his removal as coach] is long overdue. [...] The ANC will never support Jake White if he bids for a second term."

So, the Springbok rugby coach invited trouble by mixing politics with sport – clearly no amount of irony is lost on this guy.

With comparably bad timing, the South African Rugby Union saw fit to advertise for a replacement for White the week before the semifinal. Wow. It's almost like they were trying to make it harder for the Springboks to win…

Some questions for the Parliamentary Committee On Sport:

- Do you think the Springboks would have done more to unite the country if there were more non-white players involved at the World Cup but they hadn't won the tournament?
- Has Thabo Mbeki had a better PR moment this millennium than when he sat on the shoulders of the Springboks, holding the William Webb Ellis trophy?
- Should the racial demographics of a South African sporting team represent the demographics of the country or the demographics of those who play the sport?
- Why are quotas allocated by race and not ethnicity? How can a team be truly representative of South Africa if it doesn't include every group: Zulu, Xhosa, Basotho, Bapedi, Venda, Tswana etc?
- Should the black-dominated US basketball and Olympic track teams have white and Latino quotas to reflect accurately the demographics of the United States?
- Have any of you actually played sport before or are you just run-of-the-mill meddlesome politicians?
- Don't you have something better to do?

The race card

"I am a white person with a valid point to make about a black person who has acted in an improper way."

"Whitey, you are racist!"

Stop changing the topic. It is not wrong to call a black man an asshole if that's what he is. After all, assholes come in a variety of colours. As do racists.

And on that note…

Racial obsessing

A decade and a half into the Rainbow Nation, and race and racism continue to cloud every single political issue in this country, not to mention countless supposedly non-political ones.

Consider, for example, the letters to the press that the Judge Hlophe incident elicited. By all accounts, Judge President John Hlophe accepted R500,000 in improper consultation fees from Oasis Asset Management; then, without declaring his interest, he granted that company permission to sue a colleague of his on an unrelated matter. After a long-awaited Judicial Service Commission was finally made public in October 2007, Hlophe escaped facing impeachment proceedings; instead, he was effectively given a light spank about the bottom and told to continue with his business. Concerned legal groups were outraged and wrote letters to newspapers. Other concerned legal groups were outraged by these concerned legal groups' outrage and also wrote letters to newspapers.

Whether or not the appropriate punishment was meted out is neither here nor there; what is here and there is how different factions reacted to the ruling. That is to say, predictably.

First Judge Johann Kriegler (white guy) wrote that Hlophe was not fit to be a judge. His opinion was supported in an open letter by senior members of the Cape Bar Council (white guys). But Kriegler's "unsolicited attack" was criticised by the Black Lawyers Association (black guys) in another letter. Soon after, the *Cape Times* featured correspondence from both sides of the argument. On one hand, the professors in the UCT Law Faculty (mostly white guys), suggested Hlophe step down. On the other hand, expressing their support for "his Lordship", were staff members of the Cape Provincial Division, including Patrick Javu (black guy), Beauty Masimba (black chick), Babalo Jaxa X Bewana (black chick, I think) and others (mostly black chicks). See what's going on here?

One day, cases like this will be assessed on their merits alone, without the racial blinkers that inform everyone's opinion. One day…

Radio

There was a time when I used to listen to the radio – to 5fm, in particular. Tony Blewett, Kevin Savage, Barney Simon, Alex Jay. These were radio DJs who knew their music; who were genuinely entertaining; who could string consecutive sentences together without sounding like egotistical imbeciles. They were my youth, man!

But those were the days when it was still called Radio 5 (remember: "Raaaaay-deo-Fiiiiiive!") and the DJ actually chose the music. Now, if you work at 5fm, your job description evidently reads: "Ignore the really bad music; discuss the latest celeb goss; insult people; talk inane drivel with your co-presenters; work in as much shameless advertising and self-promotion as possible; tell bad jokes and think yourself really funny; pretend that listeners care that you like Formula One racing; be stupid."

Oh my, it appears I'm not 14 any more.

But it's not just 5fm. Music radio today is all about pre-programmed track listing, targeted markets and appealing to the lowest common denominator. Which is to say that listening to any commercial music station in the country is sure to drive you up the wall if you have a modicum of taste and standards. No wonder road rage is on the increase.

The alternative is talk radio. This is another of those good ideas on paper that, in practice, is a direct route to Valkenberg. The presenters generally give it a good bash, but it doesn't take long to work out that they're either scandal-mongers or complete bores. And when you finally find a decent one, there are still the callers – cretins, mostly. "Hi John, I just want to say, have you seen the beer-ad banners on Green Point Main Road? It's a disgrace! They are clearly larger than permissible regulations…"

And so it becomes clear why the iPod was invented.

Reality television
Real TV? No. Just real bad.

Retarded spelling
It used to be annoying SMS spelling and computer abbreviation that made your average copy editor want to gas himself – *C u 2nite, lol, u r gr8…*

Pls stop B4 i go crzy!

This frustrating language of impatient teenagers with no sense of etiquette or decorum was subsequently adopted by anyone with a keyboard and an IQ of under 85 – a surprisingly large percentage of the world population. But now it's got worse.

These days, the excuse of saving time or digital characters on a cellphone keypad doesn't even come into the question. People have simply become idiots. "Dis" for "this", "dat" for "that", "woz" for "was" – and so on. Why are we talking like retarded children? Are we actually devolving? Was the pinnacle of human evolution Homo Sapiens circa 1994?

Various critical events suggest that this may indeed be the case. Firstly, the World Wide Web was initially publicised in 1991; secondly, the inaugural commercial text message was sent in 1992. Most importantly, however, 1994 saw the release of the movie *Dumb And Dumber*. It was, paradoxically, cinema genius and a portent of things to come.

Wayne Rooney
Angry little man.

7/11 lighting

It's like they want to do freaking surgery in there or something. What's with all the fluorescent lights, 7/11 people? You trying to scare off the albinos or what?

SARS

Great work getting all that money into the coffers, SARS people. Just remember, we all still hate you.

Leon Schuster fans

"Imagine a guy's name is Jack. Think of how you might greet him."
  "Howzit, Jack."
  "Okay, something else."
  "*Hoesit*, Jack."
  "Not that. Try again."
  "How are you, Jack."
  "Er, no, something totally different."
  "*Molo, Jack. Uphila njani?*"
  "No. Keep it simple."
  "Hello, Jack."

"Simpler."

"'Sup, Jack!"

"First word is two letters."

"Yo, Jack."

"Begins with an H."

"Er... Hi, Jack?"

"Great! Okay, now say it fast..."

And so Leon Schuster's internal monologue with his hypothetical movie viewer surely went, before yet another enduring moment of classic South African cinema was born. The comedic possibilities of juxtapositioning a man called Jack and a criminal who announces his unlawful intentions with the line "Hijack!" are just stupendous, you'd think. Well, no actually, you might not think that. Unless you're thinking it's stupendously bad. Which it is.

And yet Leon Schuster has, for over 20 years, been entertaining South Africans with jokes of such quality, flooding movie theatres across the country with highly excited audiences since his first candid-camera hits in the mid '80s. How's this for an astonishing fact: his last three movies are all on the list of South Africa's top-ten grossing movies of all time. *Harry Potter*? *The Lord Of The Rings*? Uh-uh, my friend: *Mr Bones*. It's at number two on the list (behind that crap boat story), and it brought in R33 million in ticket sales. R33 million!

The astounding thing is that it's nearly impossible to tell Schuster's movies apart, especially if you've never watched one from start to finish – if you've just caught bits and pieces on TV, watching in awestruck fascination as you might watch, say, an obese woman showering (tip: just look away). His movies simply merge into one timeless pantheon of South African cinematic humour. One day, they will release the comprehensive Leon Schuster DVD collection called *Oh Schucks, Mama, You Must Be Joking About The Sweet And Short Zulu Mechanic Menace On My Stoep. Bone!* They'll delete all the credits in the middle and it will still make sense as a 16-hour candid-camera epic. As much sense as a stand-alone Schuster movie does, at any rate.

I don't blame Schuster. That would be like blaming Colonel Sanders for the millions of chickens reared under artificial lamps each year. The collective human desire for chickens to be placed in confined spaces with little or no sunlight was beyond the Colonel's control. Similarly, the

Schuster is merely providing for the deep-seated desire of South Africans to see imbecilic jokes rehashed by a white guy painted up as a black chick. Oh, the high jinks you can have with Afrikaner tannies when you roll meatballs under your arms! Or with sheep when you chase them around on fast-forward! Or with excitable, young black men when you say the word "gaffer" enough times.

Besides, I'm pretty sure Mr Schuster – who is, from all accounts, a genuinely nice guy – doesn't give a flying fig whether I blame him or not. He clearly knows which side his bread is buttered. He's on record as saying, "Whatever the critics and the high-faluted larney okes might say about my comedy, I have to please the man on the street. I don't care for anybody else, other than the average oke on the street."

But geez, are we that average? Apparently so. Which is why his biography will doubtless sell 25 million copies in the Free State alone, while this book will be lucky to make it off the printing press. Goddamn it.

Jackie Selebi

It's strange to think that Jackie Selebi could have connections with the sinister underworld characters of organised crime – mobsters who run protection rackets, mafia types who take out hits on people... Because Jackie Selebi looks a lot more harmless than that. You'd think he should rather be entertaining young children in the park. After all, you always see him in that cute little outfit. If you swapped his blue police hat for a red fez, you might even mistake him for an organ-grinder monkey. Solely because of his outfit (no other reason, conclusion jumpers).

That said, it might be an idea to make the next national police commissioner an organ-grinder monkey. Monkeys can't talk, so it couldn't say anything stupid like, "What's all the fuss about crime?" And it's not like the monkey could do a worse job.

Jackie Selebi, president of Interpol? Now there's a laugh.

Self-help programmes

Do we wish to know The Secret? To awaken our giant potential, or access our intuitive possibilities through meditation and positive visualisation? We do not. So fuck off, Rhonda Byrne. You and the Anthony Robbins you rode in on.

Service

Shop assistant. Not to be confused with shop dummy. Similar blank expression on face, but assistant gives herself away by moving occasionally. Often an aspiring *Idols* contestant; more concerned with how she looks and high volume of in-store music than with helping customers with purchases. Sometimes comes with a sense of humour, as when you ask if a certain item is available in another size and she answers, "I don't know, I only work here." Which, astoundingly, really does happen. (No wonder online retailers are reaping healthy profits.)

Waiter. Often a shop assistant that has moved up, noticeable by running attempts at stand-up comedy: "The starter special is mussels – but the sauce is not too… strong." You hope he's just made it up – by accident – but he's been using that line for six years. Since he dropped out of marketing college. Poor memory – often, but not necessarily, the result of drug habit. Usually a smoker, explaining the frequent absences from the room, particularly when you're waiting for the cutlery he's forgotten to bring, as your main course gets cold in front of you.

Barman. Egocentric schmodel; believes his sole employment requirement is to flair and chat up women. Below-average intelligence. Struggles to make connection between your continued presence at bar counter and his not having served you. Still waiting for big modelling break – ten years after doing his portfolio shots.

Sharks fans

I used to loathe the Sharks. It started with their collection of unbearably annoying scrumhalves – think back to Kevin Putt, Craig Davidson, Ryan Walker – and it kind of went from there. But now they've got Ruan Pienaar who is pretty cool. Not for him this metrosexual eyebrow-plucking nonsense. Respect. And that dreadful Rudi Straueli-inspired playing style seems to have disappeared for the time being. Nice work, Dick Muir.

So these days there's a semblance of regard for the buggers – which is not to say I don't celebrate joyously whenever the Sharks get knocked out of the Currie Cup or Super 14. Of course I do. Particularly if it's in the final to a last-minute Bryan Habana try that, frankly, should have been disallowed. My point is that the Sharks are no longer unbearable; it's their supporters who are.

It all started after Craig Jamieson took the Banana Boys to that famous victory over the Bulls in the 1990 Currie Cup final. He seemed like such a happy fellow, and no-one begrudged him or his team their victory – their first ever. After that, there followed several years of success, in which Natal won three more titles. During this time, the Sharks brand was born, and this is when things started going wrong: a myth quickly developed that the Sharks are and always have been the greatest team known to mankind in all the history of the universe. Ra-ra, the Sharks!

The truth of the matter is that, since the competition went annual in 1968, the Sharks have won four Currie Cups, compared with the 16 of the Bulls and ten of Western Province. Of course, they won none prior to that, when Province was cleaning up. More pertinently, they have not won a major title in more than a decade. You'd think their fans would have gained a little humility in this time; that they may have learnt that the sun does not, in fact, shine directly out of their team's rear – and yet the insufferable arrogance returns every year, even as that last 1996 trophy disappears further into the past…

Sharks fans, it's fine to drive around Joburg and Cape Town with your cute little Sharks stickers on your Citi Golfs, but it's about time you showed some respect to the locals. Stop shouting at the TV in the bar, put away the flags and the Sharks Club banner and calm the hell down. Then go on holding thumbs for that next win. It's just around the corner, promise.

Shopping-mall food halls

What's worse than a shopping mall? A shopping-mall food hall.

Take your pick from a panoply of fast-food shrines – Wimpy, Nando's, Milky Lane, a pizza slice-away, the compulsory cheap Chinese restaurant, a dodgy curry parlour – then gobble your food down from plastic containers, surrounded by oversized people sitting on undersized chairs in a grubby, neon-lit atrium that resembles more closely a prison dining hall than a respectable eating area. God, it's gross.

Even if you're eating in an official restaurant, you can be guaranteed the insane shopping-mall rental prices will have them charging you astronomical prices for microwave meals dished up by an oil-rig cook.

Given that we have the best weather in the world in South Africa, can we at least suffer our dire service and eat our substandard food while sitting in the sun?

Small-car advertising

Most people with R100,000 or so to spend on new wheels are looking to buy a pure-bred racing machine, a quite apparent fact if commercials for small cars are anything to go by. While ads for more expensive models (with genuine power and speed) focus on safety, and the warmth and fuzziness that comes with communicating with your personal transportation in an emotional way, lower-end car advertising is all about extracting extreme performance and excitement from a lawnmower engine.

Nissan Micras, Citroen C2s, Renault Clios and other glorified four-wheel motorbikes are shown in electrifying images or dominating the road with driving antics last seen in bad Paul Walker movies (and that one without him that was even worse). Mostly, the ads are shot in deserted cities at night because this is the only way you'll come close to conquering the streets in one of these cars. Or, as in the C2's case, the commercial might be illustrated because the car can't actually do what's being shown on screen – like jump bridges and dodge missiles and stuff. Never mind. The impressionable 20-year-olds will lap it up anyway!

While South Africa's road-death statistics hover around 1,000 deaths a month, advertising agencies throw the full weight of their clients' huge budgets into creating speeding Schumachers out of youngsters who've barely learnt to drive. You can picture the focus groups, run by raging-hormone scriptwriters fresh out of varsity.

BRAD: Okay, guys, we're looking for street cred. Tell us what's so hot right now.

JEROME: Racing our pimped-up rides at 3am when the streets are empty.

BRAD (NODS KNOWINGLY AND OFFERS A FREE ENERGY DRINK): Cool! And what do you guys look for in a car?

SIPHO: Anything that shits all over other cars on the road.

BRAD (WRITING FURIOUSLY): All riiiight! Does the fact you can only afford entry-level vehicles make any difference?

DAVE: Hey, all cars are still restricted to 60km/h in town, aren't they? We can still look better by ignoring the speed limit. I flew past a 5 series in my Tazz the other day. That sad bastard never saw me coming!

BRAD: I can see my awards for this campaign already! Cool! Or is it hot?*

There's a reason why 18- to 24-year-old males pay the highest insurance premiums: because they are inexperienced, overly aggressive drivers and they kill themselves a lot. Advertising agencies trying to foist the idea that their hatchbacks are just an engine tweak off Formula One performance really aren't helping the situation. Yes, Renault, we're looking at you here.

* This is not how the writers at the ad agency for Ford do their work, though. Evidently, they just drop a whole lot of acid and watch fairy tales.

Smiley faces

The story goes that the smiley face first came about in the '60s as a non-trademarked graphic for an American insurance company. Various people claim a role in its origins, but it was only popularised a decade later by a pair of brothers who used it to sell novelty items – T-shirts, pins, bumper stickers and whatnot. Interesting, right? No, not really. But harmless, at least.

Some further information, then: the first text smileys :-) and :-(were invented on 19 September 1982 by a computer nerd at Carnegie Mellon University in Pennsylvania*. Okay, still not particularly interesting. But not so harmless any more, because this event led directly to the wild proliferation of smileys in all forms of digital correspondence today. The plague is upon us.

Technically, it's the nerd's fault that text smileys came into being, but it seems they were an inevitable creation. He just happened to get there first. (Not that we should forgive him; he should be still smeared in honey and thrown to the fire ants.) The real blame lies with only one person: woman. Oh yes, woman, it is all your fault. Damn your feminine insecurities.

Women love smileys because they are, if anything, about reassurance – which, as we all know, is what women live for. You have to reassure them about everything: their clothes, their hair, the meal they've cooked, the e-mail they're reading… And so, because we've all become so hopeless at communicating, we have to attach a semicolon and closed bracket at the end of a sentence just to show we're not mad at whomever is reading it. The assumption being that without the smiley we *are* mad.

```
I hope you had a good day.
```

No smiley. Oh my god, he's being sarcastic! He really hopes I had a bad day, doesn't he? That bastard! I'm never talking to him again.

And so, when that shit-storm passes, you learn the placating effect of the smiley in communicating with women – whether it's a girlfriend, friend, colleague or client. So you start using smileys occasionally – you know, to reassure the women…

You may think this is fine, but it is not. Because the first domino has fallen. And smileys are actually little demons that eat our souls. Believe it because it's true.

Along with horrendously annoying web acronyms, such as lol (See **Lol**), fyi and imho ("in my humble opinion" – humble, my ass), smileys symbolise all that is awful about modern communication: how rushed, careless, insecure, shallow and incompetent it is. Can't be bothered to string together the appropriate words? Oh well, throw in a smiley. Who cares that I'm not really smiling at the time?

Emoticons are, of course, the next level down, and then come the absolute pits: graphic emoticons – those little faces you find on MSN and the like. Hmmm, how do I show that I'm superhappy? I know, I'll insert the very smiley face that says SUPERHAPPY underneath!

How has it come to this? These things should have age limits on them. Not permissible for people over the age of nine.

The last word is on smileys from men to men: very disturbing.

* I would like to make it clear that these two smileys are the first two I've ever written. Of course, I used them only to describe smileys, not to denote my emotion at the time. But I apologise anyway.

"Sorry"

Ag, sorry man. If there's one word every South African uses every day it's "sorry". From the frequency of its daily deployment, you'd swear we are the politest society on earth. The thing is, we aren't actually sorry at all. What we really mean is "excuse me'". But around here that's what you say when you're about to pick a fight.

South African drivers

Jesus, we're bad drivers. It's almost pathological, that's how bad we are; as though we've been given lessons in how to infuriate our fellow drivers in an attempt to increase traffic jams and road rage.

Let's start with the basics: indicating. In the rest of the world, indicating is a sign of competence in a driver. In South Africa, it is a sign of weakness. Who needs to indicate when you own the road? Instead, we have hazard lights. Want to drive in the yellow lane? Put on your hazards. Want to stop in the fast lane for a piss? Use the hazards. Reverse into oncoming traffic after missing your turn? Hazards. Fantastic little button this. There's nothing like blinking orange all around your car to indicate to surrounding motorists that you are doing exactly what you want. If anyone gives you attitude, just show them the finger and let them have it. "My hazards are on, you fool! What are you on about?!" Works every time.

Once you're confident in your inability to use indicators and your proficiency with the hazards, you can graduate on to more general driving skills. Remember: consideration is for pussies, so never let anyone in. Always run red lights. Hoot at everything. Cut through the smallest gaps possible. Speed regularly and make a point of driving right up people's arses, especially if they can't pull into the adjacent lane. The following distance is two seconds – that means you can never be more than two seconds behind the car in front. If you must drive slowly, stick in the right lane. If someone pisses you off, pursue him and beat him through his car window.

Master these skills and you'll fit right in, though to be an advanced South African driver, you need to know the art of cutting. This is what you do when a whole line of cars is backed up before an exit and you drive all the way down the line and muscle into it at the last minute. Guaranteed to boil blood and worsen the traffic jam. Great work! You're a natural!

Cutters, there is a special place in hell, right next to the circus clowns, reserved especially for you.

Sports talk shows

SuperSport is the greatest sports channel in the world. In the entire world. Let's be clear on that. Sometimes I consider SuperSport a part of the family, that's how much I love it. But even SuperSport can't get a sports talk show right.

Inevitably there is a keen (or not so keen) presenter marshalling two or three dim ex-sportsmen with a vocabulary centred on the terms "ja", "no", "definitely" and "for sure".

"Ja definitely, the team that wants it more will win."

"Ja no for sure, both teams were always going to give it 110 per cent."

"Ja no definitely for sure for sure definitely no for sure ja."

Between the lot of them, they have the combined wit, charisma and eloquence of a cartload of chimpanzees. So instead of the usual sports clichés, I'd personally prefer it if they just went, "Ooh-ooh. Aah! Aah! Aah!" and maybe jumped up and down a bit.

John Robbie's not bad, though. It's a bit inaccurate to lump him in with the chimps. He's more of a leprechaun. They should use him more.

"Struggle" excuses

No-one can ever denigrate the role of "the struggle" in South African history. It is integral to our identity as a nation.

What we can denigrate is using the struggle as an excuse for all kinds of political indulgence and shenanigans, a decade and a half into democracy. JZ sings of his machine gun – forget about the massive implications this has in a society oppressed by gun violence; it's just a struggle song, you can't take it literally… Everyone's saying Manto is a thief, a boozer and incompetent – but she was committed to the struggle for many years and will always be a hero… Mugabe's annihilating his country, destabilising our economic zone and pouring misery on his people – never forget his role in the struggle…

How about the struggle the average SA citizen has to go through to deal with all your political crap?

And what of struggle "credentials" as motivation and justification for political positions? Why should your participation in violent attacks and your ability to throw bombs into crowded bars make you a viable candidate for a municipal position of power and responsibility? Yes, politicians are a breed apart when it comes to their personal moral codes, but surely the fact that you have crossed the ethical line that involves killing innocent people makes you *less* qualified, not *more* qualified, for the job?

Take, for instance, Robert McBride. Here's a guy responsible for the car bomb that killed three people and wounded dozens more in 1986 outside Magoo's Bar in Durban – and he made a conscious decision to be responsible for it. Whether or not he was motivated by politics is besides the point: somewhere deep down in his soul, this man was at peace with the fact that he was about to murder innocent people. Is he really the best guy to be a Metro Police Chief 20 years down the line? Are we surprised that he's been involved in a drunk-driving incident, with various associated allegations of intimidation and threats, and that two of his own metro police (who were involved in removing him from the scene of his accident) had to take out court interdicts against him because they feared for their lives?

Stupid packaging

There was a time when packaging design was all about innovation and ease of use. Having evolved from woven-grass baskets and clay pots, packaging finally found a miracle material in the form of plastic. Polyethylene terephthalate was developed in the '70s and is the most commonly used packaging plastic today. Here was a substance that could safely replace those heavy and cumbersome glass and tin containers used for centuries to preserve and protect. All good and well – until someone decided that heat shrink packaging was the way to go. Companies with names like Seal-it, Shrinktec and Safety Seal sprung up to cater for this exciting innovation in technology. They should have added the words "for good" at the end of their names, since some self-amusing industrial designer obviously thought it would be a laugh if you could see the product clearly but not actually get at it. Now you need a degree in engineering just to open your plastic-wrapped purchase. Plenty of instructions inside on how to use the sealed item, but nothing on how to open the package in the first place – just a seamless plastic bubble thicker than your standard bulletproof vest. Inevitably, when you've finally claimed the item from its plastic prison, you have a table strewn with kitchen knives, scissors and possibly an angle grinder or two, and at least three fingers bleeding. And all this for a new travel plug.

24

I'm an open-minded guy. I'm up for escapism and fantasy. But we're coming up for Season 8. How many insanely bad days can one guy have?

Teenagers

It's not like teenagers were ever great. They've always been spotty little know-it-alls, all pustular and angsty. Even *they* never liked themselves.

But they've got worse.

Now, instead of disappearing to their rooms to listen to heavy-metal music on their Walkmans whenever they get the chance, modern teenagers are all out there and in your face, dressed up like gangsters and hookers – evidently the appropriate attire for lurking on street corners and outside McDonald's restaurants.

Other current teen subspecies include junk-food scoffers who live behind their computer screens and, their diametric opposite, budding professional sportsmen who've been on contract, and possibly growth hormones, since they were six. After years of regular steroid use and minimal parental discipline, this last group is not averse to randomly assaulting the local hobo when out on the prowl at night.

Can you imagine being a school teacher without recourse to corporal punishment for these little bastards? Couldn't think of anything worse.

Telemarketing-pitch preambles

"Hello, Tim speaking."

"Hello, how are you?"

"Er, fine."

"I am fine, thank you."

[Silence]

"Am I talking to Mr Rickman?"

"Mr Richman. Yes, that's me."

"Mr Rickman, my names is Agnes*, I am calling from A Large Financial Institution."

Uh-oh, must be my overdraft again.

"Yes…?"

"Is it a good time to talk?"

"Er, no, not really…"

"Before we start, I must inform you that this conversation may be recorded for quality-control purposes."

Oh Christ, it's the overdraft. Or maybe the insider trading.

"Okay…"

"Is that all right with you?"

They're on to me…

"I suppose…"

"Mr Rickman, do you worry what might happen to your family if you pass away suddenly?"

What? Aaargghh, a sales pitch! Not again!

Why can't they just open up with the pitch and stop wasting our time?

* *Agnes from Standard Bank actually called me while I was writing this. No shit.*

Telemarketing with Indian origins

But if I am going to have my time wasted by an unsolicited telephone call, I'd rather not have the accompanying guilt of knowing the guy on the other end of the line is relying on my sale to feed his 74-strong family in the slums of Calcutta, because the two cents an hour they're paying him is sure going to be bamboozling his chances there otherwise. And I'd prefer to understand what he is saying so that I know exactly what it is I have no use for before I tell him, "I'm putting down the phone now".

Telemarketing

You know what? Just leave me alone. That would solve various problems.

Telkom

If you've ever considered quantifying the badness of Telkom – with its special brand of market monopolisation, exorbitant pricing and seemingly deliberate ineptitude – take a look at its customer-service replies to the (many, many) complaints on www.hellopeter.com. Here you will discover that Telkom's ability to explosively aggravate any human being alive who comes in contact with its services is, in fact, boundless. In case you can't be bothered, we found some random samples, complete with spelling errors, farcical corporate speak and copy-and-paste customer placations:

In response to a complaint headed "Lying staff":

Sincere apologies for the inconvenience caused by the discrepancy in completing the task at hand. National Customer Care will escalate accordingly and oversee until complete.

In response to a user complaining that his ADSL line had been down for four days and he had phoned the Telkom call centre 15 times without being helped:

Apologies for the delay in restoring service to your line. National Customer Care is investigating the nature of the delay and will escalate accordingly.

In response to a complaint headed "ADSL 5 Week Saga Part 3!!!!!":

Interfacing with the Company through various mediums all at once leads to many personnel concentrating on one issue and this does have a tendency to create confusion Eg. this office is soliciting assistance from the technical environment in escalating the installtion (as per your previous posts), whilst (as per indication in this post) other personnel have been requested to cancel your order.

In response to a post complaining about "very poor service":

Sincere apologies for the delay in installing your line. Your message will be escalated via customer care and we endeavour to install as expeditiously as possible.

Anyone want to hazard a guess just how "sincere" those apologies are? Or where they came up with "escalate accordingly"? Or when someone with some influence is going to escalate a boot up Telkom's ass?

Tourists
They ruin everything.

Manto Tshabalala-Msimang
Sometimes we have doubts. Is there a god? Are Angie's breasts real? Is it wrong to demonise Manto Tshabalala-Msimang as the symbol of idiocy, unaccountability, neglect, egomania and farce in our national government? The first two may be debatable, but just to confirm the last one: no. And that's a definitive no – the same thing Dr Beetroot said for many years to AIDS sufferers asking for antiretroviral drugs.

Here's a woman who's effectively made it the defining mark of her tenure as minister of health to sentence countless South Africans to death, by (among other things) refusing to make available Nevirapine to HIV-infected mothers prior to 2003. Having begrudgingly conceded that People Who Know About Science And Stuff may, in fact, have a point when they say that antiretrovirals are vital in combating the AIDS epidemic, Manto continues to reiterate her belief that traditional medicines are the way to go. In 2006, the South African stand at the International AIDS Conference in Toronto was, effectively, a vegetable display. Is it possible to top that for a national embarrassment? Perhaps if Manto had arrived dressed up like a giant lemon? (Which would be appropriate, of course.)

Then, having garnered a modicum of sympathy – a very tiny modicum, but a modicum nonetheless – after undergoing a liver transplant, Manto's first noteworthy act back in the job was to throw her toys and withdraw from the third South African AIDS Conference, in June 2007, on discovering she had only been given a minor speaking role. Shame, Manto, are you wondering why no-one likes you? Listen closely: it's because YOU TELL PEOPLE DYING FROM AIDS TO EAT BEETROOT! WHAT THE HELL DID YOU EXPECT? By the way, how's the African potato and garlic working out in lieu of the daily cocktail of immunosuppressants you need to keep the new liver? Or are you, in fact, taking the prescribed drugs from the doctors who treated you in the nice private medi-clinic?

According to widespread reports – that were not refuted, as of February 2008 – our health minister is an alcoholic. Transplant eligibility aside, this might be considered the equivalent of having a thief in charge of the ministry of finance. Funny that, because Manto happens to have that charge hanging over her head, too. Trevor Manuel, look out.

Twenty/20 cricket

Anyone who played cricket at school has known about 20-over cricket for a long time. Longer than Twenty20 cricket has been around, that's for sure. Because they would have played it in Standard Two. When they were ten. When 40 overs per game was considered the limit to what a ten-year-old could handle.

You might think you know where this is going – a general equating of the mental capacities of the ten-year-olds of yesteryear and the morons for which Twenty20 is tailored today – and you'd be pretty much spot on. Because they really are similar. No taste, no sophistication, the attention span of a sunbird… It's almost impossible to tell them apart.

People today, as we've established elsewhere, are idiots. They want their entertainment five minutes ago, they want it louder than the explosions in the last Michael Bay movie, and they want it more colourful than the blood on their PlayStation screens. If things aren't moving at 1,000 miles an hour, they're not interested. And if they are interested, please bear in mind that it will only be for several seconds at a…

Where were we?

Oh, right. Twenty20 cricket: less a logical progression of limited-overs cricket than an imposition of the mindlessness of modern society on a once-proud sport. Subtlety traded for crudeness; skill for luck; glorious strokeplay for ugly hoiks; genuine joy for compulsory fun; general pleasantness for goddamned dancing freaks who you really just want to dive-tackle. But that would be rugby, then, wouldn't it? Ooh, there's a thought! How about we shorten it to ten overs a side and add 20 minutes of rugby afterwards? Maybe throw in a round of boxing at half-time and get some big-name golfers in for a couple of holes of putt-putt? Awesome idea!

Or is it just a complete load of shit? Shit? We're going with shit.

The UK

English-speaking white South Africans, otherwise known as *soutpiels*, have always had the indefatigable bastion of the Motherland to fall back on in desperate times. Since the 1820s, when the settlers arrived, Britain has remained the steady haven of culture and civilisation to rely on when things get all too… African down here. The pilgrimage "home" to eat strawberries and cream at Wimbledon or drink tea at Fortnum & Mason is a perennial pastime to reinvigorate the sometimes-frayed nerves that living among "the natives" can bring about. Jolly good show!

Except that the UK is now god-awful, having degenerated into a yob-ridden cesspit of politically correct war-mongering delinquents. Yo, Blair! Nice work. When Bob Mugabe openly mocks you and the universal response is, "Hmmm, Mugabe is a diseased, megalomaniac despot who has raped his country, but he makes a good a point", you know you've dropped the ball somewhere along the line. Nowadays, if you turn on Sky News and manage to get through the mandatory child kidnapping/ falling-off-balcony-while-on-holiday coverage and 30-second insert on the latest Baghdad suicide bombing (death toll: 68), you'll inevitably get to a crackdown on binge drinking and anti-social behaviour in Manchester, followed by an update on the latest teen murder in east London. Excuse me, chaps, but mindless gun crime is our speciality, what. This is *not* why we make the trip over. In fact, now that you can get executed on the tube for wearing a jacket and looking vaguely tanned, those of us with a touch of the tar-brush are thinking of going to Plett instead.

The British used to be sensible and practical, killing two birds with one stone when drinking gin and tonic for medicinal purposes, for example. That was just smart. Now they sing "Baa, baa, rainbow sheep" and write "Deferred success" on children's term reports rather than "Failed" – because they don't want to offend anyone. That's just stupid.

The British used to be cultured and sporting. Now they give us *Pop Idols* and crappy girl groups, they think footballers' weddings are the ultimate entertainment, and they are the world's most painful winners if they happen to fluke a soccer or rugby victory (another reason to be grateful for the Boks).

The British used to be a gentlemanly folk, too polite even to think about putting you out. Now the average Pom is an 18-year-old velour tracksuit-wearing chav, pregnant with her second kid so she can qualify for welfare housing, who gets fall-over drunk on alcopops and shames sailors with her language.

Oh Motherland, what happened? Seems like just the other day you were the pinnacle of civilisation, and now you're just crap. At least the weather hasn't changed – it's still utter shite.

Under-eye serum for men

Just how far are we going to go with this metrosexual business? Bit of hair gel, fair enough. Face wash, no problem. Hell, exfoliate if you must. Even moisturiser for the sensitive-skin Sandton boys is semi-acceptable. Joburg air is dry, your skin gets all chapped… You probably shouldn't be on map duty, but fine, at a push, we'll give you the moisturiser.

But under-eye serum for men? What the hell is going on here? If you're not sure what we're talking about – and good on you, boychee, go scratch your balls and crack yourself another ale – this is the skin product that has been marketed as such: "You think you look good. She thinks you look more repulsive than a turd breakfast." Or words to that effect.

Time out for a second. Let's give this a run through the logic-o-meter. Isn't manipulative, prey-on-insecurities advertising like this usually the exclusive domain of women's markets? And aren't men not women? Therefore men shouldn't be susceptible to this, right? Right?

And yet there are the eye serums and eye gels on the shelf in Stuttafords, alongside various other skin hydrators and all-over body creams for men. If he looks hard enough these days, a man can even find male make-up…

Guys, there's a line. Moisturiser is close to the line. A pink shirt is close to the line. But under-eye serum is not near the line, okay? It's over the fucking horizon. Right next to facials, back-sack-and-crack waxes and the girly-man club.

"Up next" boxes on TV

Here comes the climax of the M-Net movie, the conclusion of two hours' viewing… and, like clockwork, up pops the box in the corner, advertising the next show. Television channels love this marketing opportunity; whether it's a prime-time programme or a late-night movie, you're assured to have that little box distracting you ever so slightly from the healthy validation that the denouement you've been eagerly awaiting should have offered. Now, instead of being entirely satisfied with what you've been watching, a little part of your brain – that little Easily Distracted part that went "Hey, what's that up there in the corner?" – is not happy. He's going, "What the hell, man! I think I missed something!" And the In-Charge part of your brain's saying, "Relax, dude, you didn't miss anything." And he's going, "Uh-uh, I missed something. That was indecent, man! It was an invasion of our privacy!" And that gets In-Charge thinking, "Goddamn it, the little bastard's right. That was not cool. What is wrong with these people that they have to market their produce to me at every available moment? I'm already watching their channel!" And the little guy butts in with, "They'll only be happy when they have our soul!" And now In-Charge is really ticked off and says to the Conviction part of your brain, "Hey, Conviction, I think we should do something about this. You know, make a point of not watching the next show as a protest." And Conviction says, "Nah, I'm not really into that idea. Let Grudge take care of it." So you sit back and get ready for the next show, which you were going to watch anyway, and that little Grudge part of your brain files it away with everything else in the world that's pissing you off.

M-Net, for the sake of your viewers' mental health, please stop doing this. We're sad enough to be watching *Brothers & Sisters* as it is – and we are going to check the on-screen info to find out what's coming up next, promise.

Verimark commercials

You'd think that a Verimark commercial would do the exact opposite of what it sets out to do; that is, you'd think that anyone who watches a Verimark commercial would roll around in crushed glass and bathe in lemon juice before actually buying a Verimark product. And yet the Verimark commercials keep coming and, by all accounts, the Verimark products keep selling. Very suspicious. Selective on-screen hypnosis or something. Maybe it's a cult.

Vigilante justice

It's not so much the vigilante justice that's bad, as the necessity for it.

Violent student protests

Hey, guys. The university has announced it's raising the tuition fees. What shall we do? Protest peacefully, present our complaints to the relevant authority and maintain the moral high ground? Or revel in the delicious irony of causing even more university expenses by burning tyres, destroying campus buildings and stoning motorists, many of whom quite possibly have absolutely nothing to do with the university, let alone its administration and fee structuring?

Bear in mind that these are university students who have to make this call – people who have passed matric and evidently possess the intelligence to study at a tertiary institution… And yet, several times a year, a South African campus erupts with violence and mayhem as bands of toyi-toyiing students protest furiously over some or other grievance. Usually it's the result of increased fees, sometimes it's because student-council bodies happen not to like each other and, on occasion, it's because the university has had the temerity to fail people. The cheek! Standard MO is to disrupt classes, break windows and intimidate faculty staff, although students have been known to graduate (ha-ha) to other activities.

In October 2005, for example, students at the University Of Zululand petrol-bombed their dining hall and caused R1.2 million of damage. Five were charged with attempted murder, intimidation and vandalism. And in October 2007, more than 40 University Of Johannesburg students were arrested for, among other things, throwing bottles, fire extinguishers and bed frames out of residence windows at police. Unsurprisingly, four of them were shot with rubber bullets. Equally unsurprisingly, the students protested about being shot with rubber bullets. What degrees are these people getting?

Today's violent students, tomorrow's leaders…

The Vodacom meerkat

The customer brief for the Vodacom meerkat campaign must have been a hoot.

"Guys, Vodacom needs a hideously annoying character to symbolise the brand and serve as a mental punching bag for people across the nation."

"But they've already got that phenomenally dislikeable and culturally offensive George. Who could have thought 'M3P' could rub you up so badly?"

"Apparently, he's not annoying enough."

"Not annoying enough? That's impossible."

"No. They want to take annoying to… the next level."

"Whoa man, that's crazy talk."

Apparently it's called Mo. As in Mo the meerkat. Mo the motherfucker, more like.

Vuvuzelas

"Hmmm," the guy who invented the vuvuzela must have thought upon the birth of his creation, "this is pretty cool. I wonder if people will like it?" Unfortunately, they did. Some of them, at least.

"Warm regards"

It seems that plain old "Regards" at the end of an e-mail just isn't good enough any more. Even "Kind regards" doesn't cut it. No, modern e-mail etiquette demands that you're not imparting enough regards to your intended recipient unless they are "Best regards" or, at the very least, "Warm regards".

It seems fairly reasonable to assume that this moronic little trend is the work of agents, what with agents being the perpetrators of evil throughout the world and all (see **Agents**). With that in mind, "Best regards" can only be the creation of a particularly keen recruitment agent out to prove just how good he is. His finder's fee is also likely to be the "best".

"Warm regards" is trickier to pinpoint, though. Perhaps a travel agent got confused – as happens – somewhere along the line. "Have a nice holiday I hope the weather is warm regards Cheryl."

Or maybe a PR agent came up with it on purpose to differentiate her agency's regards from the bog-standard regards of everyone else. "Warm regards!! Ooh, what a great idea!!!!!!!!" Equally plausible.

If it was the PR agency's fault, rest assured there will be further qualifications in due course – temperate, hot and even boiling regards can't be too far off. Maybe it's time to get ahead of the game and start signing everything "Blistering regards" from now on. Or "Fuck you".

Wellness

Welcome to our Earth Centre of Healing and Wellness. Like shuwow, man!

"Wellness" is a nice concept, it really is, but there's something way too hippy about the word. Like a bunch of hippies in Hippyland took some hippy drugs and decided to come up with the hippiest word in the world. It makes me want to be violent, which is, at the very least, a paradox. So they should change it.

Kobus Wiese

The worst rugby commentator ever? Well no, that's probably a tie between Mac "Just-Just" Masina and Warren Brosnihan (notorious for the line, "Andries Bekker is so tall he must have been born on a long weekend"). But Kobus is everywhere. Not just in physical terms – he's a big guy, he's *everywhere* – but in terms of rugby coverage. How do the SuperSport managers justify this? Are they blinded by his launch-pad haircut and oversized suits? Or does he threaten to beat them up? And why is he speaking English most of the time? He's Afrikaans, for crying out loud. At the very least, let him impart his limited opinions in his first language.

Perhaps this is all a bit harsh. After all, Kobus has everything a rugby pundit needs – barring looks, style, insight, eloquence, clarity, wit and the ability to interview foreigners without coming across as a colossal meat-head. Which is to say, he can hold a microphone and talk at the same time.

Amy Winehouse

"Banging on about your drug habits is a bit old fart, isn't it?" These are the words of no lesser mortal than John Lydon, a.k.a. Johnny Rotten of the Sex Pistols, referring, in a 2007 interview, to Pete Doherty and Amy Winehouse, who have been known to indulge together – to the point of coma. Doherty is just a freak who no-one can take seriously (can you actually name one of his songs?), but Winehouse is an influential artist who actually sells lots of albums. Hence she might want to think about Johnny's advice and reconsider some of her lyrics. Because, unfortunately, people listen to them.

Wireless broadband download rates

"Up to 2MB/s" the advertising might say. Which, translated, means, "There was that one time that one of our technicians was standing next to the transmitter tower in perfect atmospheric conditions and briefly transferred information at a rate of 2MB/s. But usually you'll get a tenth of that. Hell, consider yourself lucky if you have reception."

When you're running around your bedroom with your laptop above your head, trying to reconnect to your online poker game because you have a pair of aces and you're about to be folded automatically – well, that's not 2MB/s.

Xylophones
Actually they're not that bad. But at least that's X out of the way.

Tony Yengeni

Tony Yengeni: the luckiest scumbag around – or so you may think. After being busted for defrauding parliament and sentenced to four years in prison for receiving a discounted Mercedes-Benz 4x4 from an arms dealer, Yengeni gets a hero's send-off from ANC officials, a jail experience that closely resembles a spa getaway, and 90 per cent of his prison sentence commuted. Having served five months of a four-year sentence, he's back out on the streets – technically unemployed, yes, but most likely greasing the wheels for a quiet return to politics.

If you're Tony Yengeni, though, chances are you don't think you're quite such a lucky scumbag. Chances are you're wondering why you had to be the fall guy and why you're running along trying to catch up as the gravy train disappears into the distance. (Those Armani suits are not designed for exercise!) Considering the European Aeronautic Defence And Space Company "rendered assistance" to 30 or so senior government officials to obtain luxury cars, according to the BBC, you can rest assured Tony is, in actual fact, a bitter ex-convict.

The bitterer, the better. Except that doesn't help with the fact that corruption and bribery is apparently the way of life at so many levels of South African governance. Oh well, at least you can buy your way out of a speeding fine these days. They really are insanely expensive!

The Zim crisis

So much has been said by so many respected political commentators, activists and leaders about just what an evil, murderous, corrupt, destructive dictator Robert Mugabe is, and how he is irreparably damaging Zimbabwe and the economy of southern Africa, that it seems futile to add much more. So we'll just call him a big poopy head and hope that the Americans discover oil there soon.

"Zulu" roots that aren't really that Zulu at all

"I went in search of my roots and had my DNA tested, and I am a Zulu." These are the words of talk-show icon Oprah Winfrey, said to about 3,200 people at a seminar in Johannesburg in June 2005 – shortly before she endorsed the Spur and Nando's.

Considering Zulu ancestry makes up roughly zero per cent of the original African-American population, this was quite a revelation at the time. Unsurprisingly, Oprah had her sceptics. "I hate to tell Oprah this, but she is sorely mistaken," Mangosuthu Buthelezi is quoted as saying. Perhaps he thought "Bullshit alert! Bullshit alert!" was unbecoming of a tribal chief.

Since the pronouncement of her Zulu heritage, it has been established that Oprah's ancestry can, in fact, be traced back to tribes that are clustered in modern-day Liberia and Zambia. So that's that cleared up, then.

Whatever her heritage, there is no refuting that Oprah is a modern American, wise in the ways of commercial success. Next time she's back in South Africa, you may find she's Shaka's grandniece returning to proclaim her empire. Then she'll try sell another burger.

Jacob Zuma

And so we come to the end of the list – to JZ. One-time chairperson of the South African National AIDS Council. He of the stupefying showering-after-having-sex-with-an-HIV-positive-woman comment.

This is yet another entry that could extend to book length, and doubtless it will over the years. Many times over. Unfortunately, we have a page limit, plus our humourless libel lawyer's hourly rate is just exorbitant, so, for the sake of practicality, we're going to have to pare it down to the basic problems.

Besides the fact that the guy always happens to have left his machine gun behind – you'd think he'd just keep it on him at all times and avoid all the bad press – there are five things about Jacob Zuma that are really rather worrying.

1. The first problem is his huge volume of support and the troublesome fact that the will of the masses is what counts at the end of the political day. For all the controversies and court cases and stupefying showering-after-having-sex-with-an-HIV-positive-woman comments, there are many people, perhaps even a majority, who think that making a cross next to JZ's name is the right thing to do. This may be a very, very scary thought to contemplate, but who's to say how others should vote? And let's be honest, it's not like he's up against a couple of Madibas and an Abraham Lincoln. Is he – shudder – perhaps the best option? Well, no, clearly not, but hopefully you get the point.

2. Second is his public acknowledgement of at least 18 kids by nine different women. That just messes with your head. And perhaps says something about his leadership-responsibility potential.

3. The third is his propensity for taking to court writers who say nasty things about him. Call him dishonest, corrupt, incompetent, ignorant, a misogynist, the "South African Dubya", a bad dancer – call him anything, almost – and you just can't expect to get away with it. So much for freedom of speech. A mere comment on the odd shape of his head can be enough to warrant court papers. It is even said that you cannot write the words "Jacob Zuma" and "buffoon" in the same sentence without being sued.

4. The fourth is directly related to the third: I would really, really like to write the words "Jacob Zuma" and "buffoon" in the same sentence. Pity.

5. The fifth and final problem is the stupefying showering-after-having-sex-with-an-HIV-positive-woman comment. How could it not be?

Anyway, off to see the libel lawyer now. God save us!

ALSO BY TWO DOGS...

Rogue Male

By Tom Rymour
Rogue Male: A Survival Guide For
The Newly Single Male is a witty and
insightful blend of social observation,
scabrous anecdotes, evolutionary
psychology and practical advice for the
newly single male – particularly those
coming out of long-term relationships.
In South Africa, with a divorce rate
around 50 per cent, this is very timely
advice indeed…

"A clever, witty and wonderfully South
African guide on how to go about
getting a woman" – *Drum*

ISBN 978 192013 721 2

Why I'll Never Live In Oz Again

By Andrew Donaldson,
Josef Talotta, Rick Crosier,
John Wardall and Tim Richman
A pro-SA take on life in our five top
emigration destinations – Australia,
New Zealand, the UK, the US and
Canada – from five South African
journalists who've been there and
done that. The updated edition
includes recent author interviews
and a new preface.

"A wonderful reminder about green
grass and the other side and the
sets of problems one exchanges in a
bid to run away" – *Natal Mercury*

ISBN 978 192013 706 8

ALSO BY TWO DOGS...

Defending The Caveman
By Tim Plewman

Finally, the world's most successful
comedy stage show has been turned
into a book... SA's original caveman
captures the wit and insight of the
play's script as he gets to grips with the
fundamental differences that separate
men and women – and he adds the
knowledge that nine years of staging
it has brought him, as well as some of
the more memorable moments that
occurred along the way.

"Plewman has taken Rob Becker's hit
battle-of-the-sexes one-man comedy
and made it his own" – *The Citizen*

ISBN 978 192013 719 9

Some Of My Best Friends Are White
By Ndumiso Ngcobo

A best-selling collection of satirical
essays on modern South African
issues from the point of view of a
successful corporate professional
– who just happens to be Zulu.
Crossing various controversial and
confusing racial divides, the book
delivers a healthy dose of black
– and white – humour.

"Hard hitting, delightfully insightful
and funny... Saying it as it is,
Ngcobo stomps across the colours
lines with impunity, kicking holy
cows out the way" – *The Citizen*

ISBN 978 192013 718 2

FOR MORE INFORMATION ON TWO DOGS VISIT
www.twodogs.co.za